Wildlife Watcher

Published in the United States by
QEB Publishing, Inc.
3 Wrigley, Suite A
Irvine, CA 92618
www.qeb-publishing.com

Library of Congress Cataloging-in-
Publication Data

Jennings, Terry J.
  Birds / Terry Jennings.
    p. cm. -- (QEB wildlife watchers)
  Includes index.
  ISBN 978-1-59566-758-8 (hardcover)
  1. Birds--Juvenile literature. I. Title.
  QL676.2.J46 2010
  598--dc22
                2009005881
Jennings, Terry J.
  Bugs / Terry Jennings.
  1. Invertebrates--Juvenile literature.
  2. Insects--Juvenile literature. I. Title. II.
Series: QEB wildlife watchers.
  QL362.4.J46 2010
  595.7--dc22
                2009005882
Jennings, Terry J.
  Small mammals / Terry Jennings.
  1. Mammals--Miscellanea--Juvenile
literature. I. Title.
  QL706.2.J46 2010
  599--dc22
                2009005884
Jennings, Terry J.
  Plants / Terry Jennings.
  1. Flowers--Juvenile literature. 2. Plants--
Juvenile literature. I. Title. II. Series.
  QK49.J384 2010
  580--dc22
                2009005883

Author Terry Jennings
Consultant Steve Parker
Project Editor Eve Marleau
Designer Liz Wiffen

Associate Publisher Zeta Davies
Editorial Director Jane Walker

ISBN 978 1 59566 907 0

Printed and bound in China

Picture credits
Key: t=top, b=bottom, r=right, l=left,
c=center
Alamy 7tr Harry Taylor, 21l blickwinkel/
MeulvanCauteren 41b Andrew Darrington,
47r Curt and Cary Given, 63b wildlife
GmbH, 63r Dave Bevan, 64t blickwinkel/
Delpho, 67t D.Robert Franz, 72b Arco
Images/ Reinhard, H., 73c tbkmedia.
de, 81b McPHoto/WoodyStock, 81t
Andrew Darrington, 82r Renee Morris,
85r WildPictures, 86r Terry Fincher.
Photo Int,, 91t Martin Hughes-Jones, 91c
Michael Grant, 103l Emilio Ereza, 105l
David Chapman, 105r blickwinkel/Jagel,
106r Nigel Cattlin, 107l Nigel Cattlin, 107r
blickwinkel/Jagel, 109c Nigel Cattlin, 109l
Huw Evans, 110t Helene Rogers, 111b
Renee Morris
DK Images 29l Dave King
IStock 56b johnandersonphoto
NHPA 13l N A Callow, 15t Laurie
Campbell, 15c Joe Blossom, 29t Stephen
Dalton, 29t Eric Soder, 29b Image Quest
3-D, 34r Martin Harvey, 39c Manfred
Danegger, 43t Alan Williams, 43b Laurie
Campbell, 44c Bill Coster, 45t Bill Coster,
48c Jaanus Jarva, 49t Bill Coster, 49b
Richard Kuzminski, 51l Rupert Buchele,
52c Lee Dalton, 57r David Tipling, 58t
Martin Harvey, 59l Martin Wendler, 59r
Martin Harvey, 79t Mark Bowler, 85b Alan
Williams, 86t Michael Leach and Meriel
Lland, 97r Ernie Janes, 99r Image Quest
3-D, 111r Guy Edwardes
Photolibrary 15b, 30b Andoni Canela,
61r Mark Hamblin, 67c Brian Kenney, 70c
Juniors Bildarchiv, 80l Mark Hamblin, 94l
Mauro Fermariello
Shutterstock 4-5 PhotoLiz, 5r
Cre8tive Images, 6t Robert Taylor, 6b
Alex Kuzovlev, 6-7c Dusty Cline, 7tc
Yaroslav, 7b Steve McWilliam, 8-9t
Johanna Goodyear, 8-9c Morgan Lane
Photography, 11t Steve McWilliam, 11c
Lepas, 12c Cre8tive Images, 13c Robert
Taylor, 13r Yaroslav, 15b Christian
Musat, 16l Joseph Calev, 16r Yellowj, 17c
Palto, 17r Dole, 18t Florin Tirlea, 18c
Studiotouch, 19b Dave Massey, 20c Kurt G,
21b Andrey Pavlov, 21r Andrey Armyagov,
22-23 vnlit, 23r Kurt G, 24-25t Joseph

Calev, 25rt Joseph Calev, 25rb Joseph
Calev, 25bl Steve McWilliam, 26c Alex
Kuzovlev, 27c Christopher Tan Teck Hean,
27b Scott Rothstein, 29b Dusty Cline,
28-29b Christoph Weihs, 28b design56,
30t Lucio Tamino Hollander Correia,
31t vera bogaerts, 31c Dave Massey,
31r Tiplyashin Anatoly, 32r iofoto, 33r
iNNOCENt, 34c Steve Byland, 35c
Christopher Ewing, 35b Milos Luzanin,
36r Morgan Lane Photography, 37l
David Dohnal, 38r iNNOCENt, 39t Tony
Campbell, 40c Andrew Williams, 40b
W. Woyke, 41tdr. Le Thanh Hung, 41r
Santiago Cornejo, 41b Christian Musat,
42c David Dohnal, 45b Hydromet, 46r
Ivonne Wierink, 47l Gertjan Hooijer,
50c Uwe Ohse, 51r Verena Lüdemann,
51b Peter Elvidge, 53t Kenneth William
Caleno, 53b Joel Calheiros, 54r iofoto, 25t
Tom Curtis, 55b David Dohnal, 57c Jason
Vandehey, 57b Timothey Kosachev,
60t gallimaufry, 62l Nik Niklz, 63c
David Hilcher, 63l Ultrashock, 65b Emily
Veinglory, 66r Eric Isselée, 68l Dwight
Smith, 69b ajt, 73t Ronnie Howard,
74c Herbert Kratky, 76c Keith Naylor,
78c Oleg Kozlov & Sophy Kozlova,
83c Tramper, 84l javarman, 84r
gallimaufry, 86-87 Pixinstock, 89r Anette
Linnea Rasmussen, 91l Anette Linnea
Rasmussen, 91r ansem, 92r Xalanx,
93t Petrova Olga Vladimirovna, 93l Gertjan
Hooijer, 100r Anette Linnea Rasmussen,
101l Saied Shahin Kiya, 101r Graeme
Dawes, 102l Hallgerd, 102r Ronald van
der Beek, 103c Gordana Sermek,
103b Martin Green, 104c Kokhanchikov,
108c Alistair Scott, 111l Daniel Gale,
112-113 iofoto, 112t R. S. Ryan, 113l Peter
Guess, 114-115 Mark Smith, 114l rebvt,
29t Roger Dale Pleis,
Science Photo Library 109cr Kathy
Merrifield/ Science Photo Library
StockXchange 10-11 Peranandham
Ramaraj, 10-11 Dawn Allynn, 24-25
Stephen Eastop, 50-51 ElvisSantana,
58-59 Kriss Szkurlatowski, 70-71 tome213,
76-77 andres_ol, 95t ks, 104b mrscenter

The words in **bold**
are explained in the
glossary on page 116.

Wildlife Watcher

Terry Jennings

QEB Publishing

Contents

Bugs

Birds

Small mammals

Plants

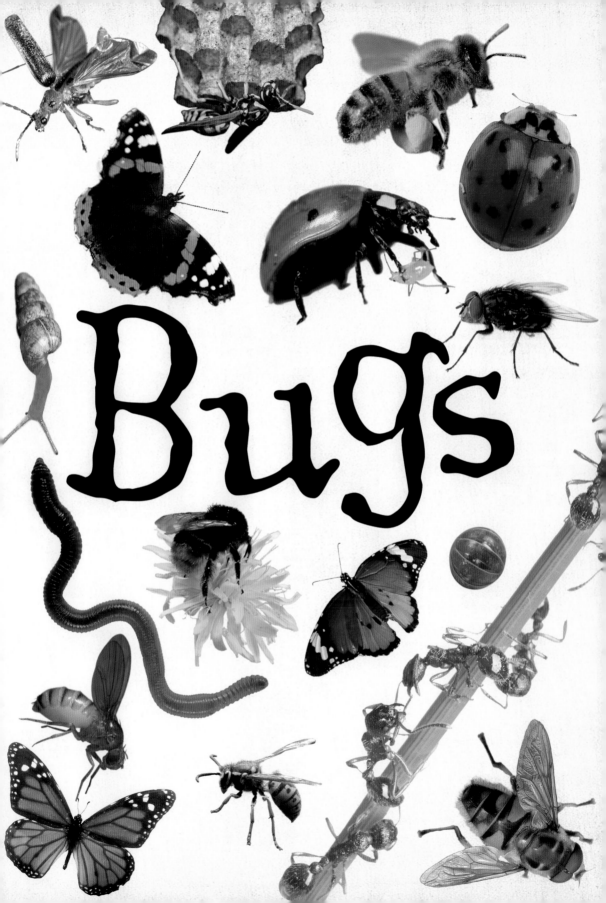

Bugs

What is a bug?

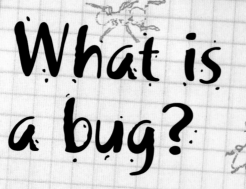

Bugs are some of the smallest animals in the world. Whether you live in the countryside or in a city, there are always bugs somewhere nearby. They live on land, in water and soil, and even in our homes.

Cranefly

Beetle

Butterfly

Slug

No backbone

Scientists call bugs by their proper name, which is **invertebrate** animals. They are small animals that do not have a backbone inside their body. Some bugs, such as snails and beetles, have a shell or hard wings to protect them. Others, such as earthworms, have no protection at all.

Earthworm

Snail

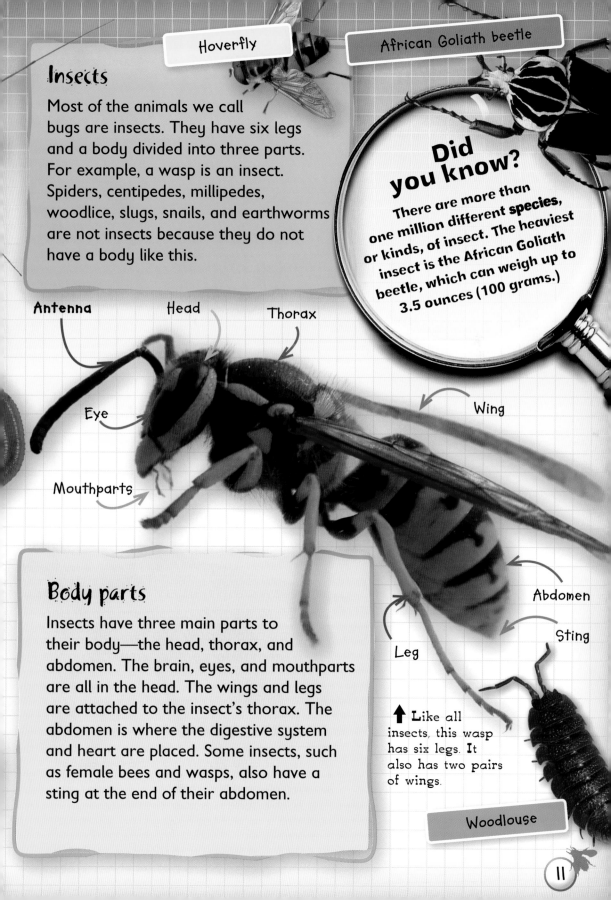

Insects

Most of the animals we call bugs are insects. They have six legs and a body divided into three parts. For example, a wasp is an insect. Spiders, centipedes, millipedes, woodlice, slugs, snails, and earthworms are not insects because they do not have a body like this.

Did you know?

There are more than one million different **species**, or kinds, of insect. The heaviest insect is the African Goliath beetle, which can weigh up to 3.5 ounces (100 grams.)

Antenna

Head

Thorax

Eye

Wing

Mouthparts

Body parts

Insects have three main parts to their body—the head, thorax, and abdomen. The brain, eyes, and mouthparts are all in the head. The wings and legs are attached to the insect's thorax. The abdomen is where the digestive system and heart are placed. Some insects, such as female bees and wasps, also have a sting at the end of their abdomen.

Abdomen

Sting

Leg

⬆ Like all insects, this wasp has six legs. It also has two pairs of wings.

Woodlouse

Be a bug hunter

Bugs are quite small, so you need to get close to them to see all their details. This should be avoided with bugs that sting, such as bees and wasps. One way to get a good look at bugs is to use a magnifying glass or hand lens.

The bug-hunter's collecting kit

These are the main tools you will need for bug hunting:
- Magnifying glass
- Plastic jars and margarine or ice-cream cartons, with air-holes in the lids
- Small paintbrushes and plastic spoons for picking up bugs without hurting them
- Notebook
- Pen or pencil
- Colored crayons

⬇ A magnifying glass lets you see small things much more clearly.

⬆ Plastic jars are good if you can make little air-holes in the lid.

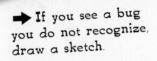 If you see a bug you do not recognize, draw a sketch.

Keeping records

Every bug hunter needs a notebook, some pencils, and colored crayons. Once you have found a bug you can put its details in a table.

Date	Type of bug	Time of day	Place	Kind of weather	Where was the bug?	What was the bug doing?
April 28	Honey bee	11 a.m.	In the park	Sunny	On snapdragon flower	Collecting pollen
May 2	Ant	3.20 p.m.	Sidewalk	Sunny	In cracks in sidewalk	Carrying sand
July 18	Snail	6 p.m.	Backyard	Raining	On cabbage plant	Feeding on leaf

WARNING!

Do not touch any bug with your bare hands. Release a bug when you have studied it. Always make sure an adult knows where you are.

Butterflies and moths

Both butterflies and moths have four wings. The front pair are called the **forewings**. The wingspan is the distance between the wing tips.

Watch it!

Record which colors and kinds of flower you see butterflies and moths feeding from. Do they have a favorite kind of flower?

Am I mostly black with orange or red bands on my wings? Do I have white marks on my forewings?

Orange or red band

White marks

Spotting butterflies and moths

- There are about 20,000 different kinds of butterfly and 100,000 species of moth.

- Butterfly and moth eggs hatch into caterpillars before they turn into adults. Caterpillars look like worms and have many legs. They can be many different colors, and even have spikes to stop birds from eating them.

- You can tell a butterfly from a moth by looking at its wings when it lands. Most moths land with their wings flat. Butterflies usually hold their wings together, above their body.

Red admiral butterfly

Wingspan: 2.5 in (64 mm)
Food: Nectar from flowers and juices from fruits
Habitat: Almost anywhere with flowers or stinging nettles
Eggs: Laid on leaves such as nettles

Am I active in the daytime? Am I mainly black with red markings?

Red markings

Cinnabar moth

Wingspan: 1.7 in (45 mm)
Food: Nectar from flowers
Habitat: Backyards, parks, waste ground, and farmland
Eggs: Laid on the underside of leaves such as ragwort and groundsel

Am I mainly white? Do my forewings have black spots and black tips?

Black tip

Black spot

Am I active at night? Do I have tiger-like white stripes on my forewings?

Cabbage white butterfly

Wingspan: 2.5 in (64 mm)
Food: Nectar from flowers
Habitat: Near plants
Eggs: Laid on the underside of leaves such as cabbages and cauliflowers

White stripes

Tiger moth

Wingspan: 3 in (76 mm)
Food: Nectar from flowers
Habitat: Backyards, parks, and waste ground
Eggs: Laid on the underside of leaves such as nettles and weeds

Flies

Flies are insects. There are more than 120,000 different kinds of fly in the world. People think that flies are a pest because they buzz around food, and a few can bite. Most flies are actually useful and harmless.

Did you know?

The wings of flies beat very fast. Those of a housefly beat about 200 times a second, a mosquito about 600 times a second, and a midge about 1,000 times a second.

Large eye

Am I medium sized and mainly dark blue or black with large eyes?

Spotting flies

🪰 Flies have only two proper wings. Their back wings, which are very small, are used for balance as they fly.

🪰 All flies lay eggs, which hatch into grubs or maggots. After spending some time feeding, the grubs turn into **pupae**, and then into adults.

Housefly

Length: 0.3 in (8 mm)
Food: Almost any kind of food, including human food, rotten fruit, and the contents of trash cans, animal droppings
Habitat: Everywhere
Eggs: Laid in manure or waste food or in soil

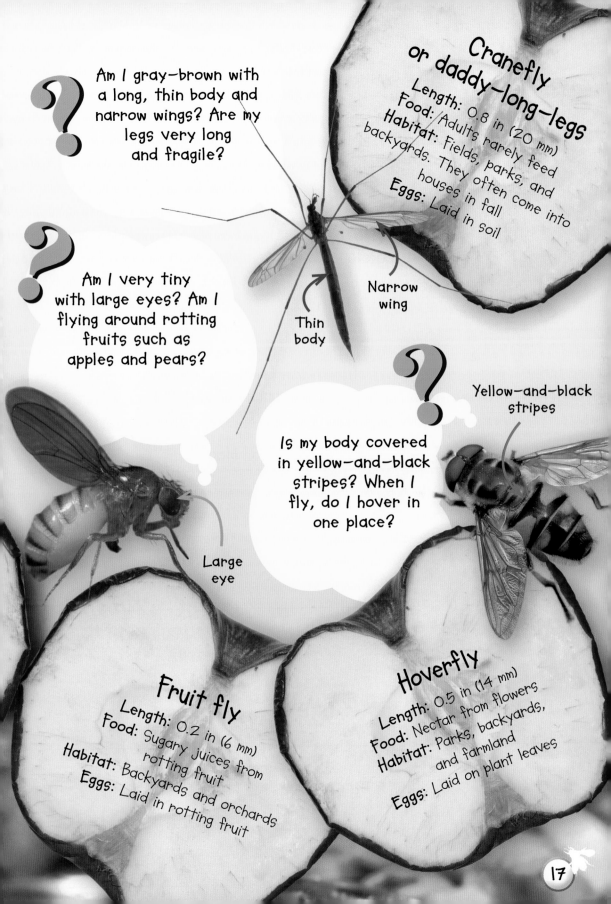

? Am I gray-brown with a long, thin body and narrow wings? Are my legs very long and fragile?

Cranefly or daddy-long-legs
Length: 0.8 in (20 mm)
Food: Adults rarely feed
Habitat: Fields, parks, and backyards. They often come into houses in fall
Eggs: Laid in soil

? Am I very tiny with large eyes? Am I flying around rotting fruits such as apples and pears?

Narrow wing

Thin body

Yellow-and-black stripes

? Is my body covered in yellow-and-black stripes? When I fly, do I hover in one place?

Large eye

Fruit fly
Length: 0.2 in (6 mm)
Food: Sugary juices from rotting fruit
Habitat: Backyards and orchards
Eggs: Laid in rotting fruit

Hoverfly
Length: 0.5 in (14 mm)
Food: Nectar from flowers
Habitat: Parks, backyards, and farmland
Eggs: Laid on plant leaves

Beetles

There are more than 370,000 different kinds of beetle in the world. They are found almost everywhere. It is easy to recognize beetles because, unlike other insects, they are covered with tough **wing cases** that look like armor. These cases are the beetle's forewings.

Did you know?

When a bee collects nectar from a flower, oil beetle grubs cling to it so they are taken back to the hive. Then the beetle grubs pretend to be bee grubs so they can feed on eggs and honey in the hive.

Am I quite small with a narrow body and long antennae? Is my thorax red or black?

Narrow body

Red thorax

Spotting beetles

 The back wings of beetles are large and papery. When beetles fly, the forewings are held upward and only the back wings flap.

Some beetles eat flesh, such as that of other insects. Many more beetles feed on plants and animal dung.

Soldier beetle

Length: About 0.3 in (10 mm)
Food: Small insects
Habitat: In large flowers and on the surface of soil
Eggs: Laid in groups in soil

Long antenna

Am I long and black
or dark blue?
Do I have long
antennae?

Ground beetle

Length: 0.6 in (16 mm)
Food: Other insects
Habitat: On the ground among
dead leaves and under logs
and stones
Eggs: Laid on the ground
or just below the surface
of soil

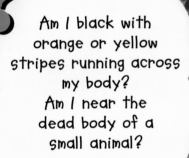

Am I black with
orange or yellow
stripes running across
my body?
Am I near the
dead body of a
small animal?

Sexton beetle

Length: 0.6 in (16 mm)
Food: The flesh of
dead animals
Habitat: Near dead animals
Eggs: Laid in the bodies
of dead animals

Orange stripe

Ridges

Am I black with
short antennae?
Do I have ridges
running along
my body?

Dung beetle

Length: 1 in (25 mm)
Food: The dung or droppings
of animals
Habitat: In grassland and
where animals such as cows,
horses, and rabbits leave
their droppings
Eggs: Laid in animal droppings

Ladybugs

Ladybugs are probably the best known beetles. Gardeners and farmers like them because they eat pests, such as greenfly and blackfly, that damage the plants in gardens and on farms.

Am I small with short legs? Are my wing cases yellow or orange with black spots, one on each wing case?

← A ladybug will eat large numbers of harmful greenfly and blackfly every day.

Short leg

Large, black spot

Spotting ladybugs

 Ladybugs are usually brightly colored with dark spots. There are about 5,000 different kinds of ladybug in the world. Each kind has a different pattern and number of spots.

🐞 If a ladybug is attacked, it will squirt out nasty-smelling blood to protect itself.

🐞 In winter, ladybugs hide away and **hibernate**, or sleep, until the warmer weather returns.

Two-spot ladybug

Length: 0.2 in (6 mm)
Food: Tiny insects such as greenfly and blackfly
Habitat: Parks, backyards, farmland, woodland, waste ground
Eggs: About 20 eggs laid on the underside of leaves of plants that are full of greenfly and blackfly

14-spot ladybug

Length: 0.1 in (5 mm)
Food: Mainly greenfly
and blackfly
Habitat: Backyards,
farmland, woodland,
waste ground
Eggs: 20–50 eggs laid on
the underside of plants
leaves that are full of
greenfly and blackfly

Am I red or
yellow with about
14 black spots,
or black with
about 14 yellow
or red spots?

Do I have short
legs? Are my wing
cases yellow or
orange with
black spots?
Are the spots
almost square?

Red wing
case

Seven-spot
ladybug

Length: About 0.3 in (8 mm)
Food: Mainly greenfly
and blackfly
Habitat: Backyards,
farmland, woodland,
waste ground
Eggs: Up to 200 eggs
on the underside of leaves
of plants that are full of
greenfly and blackfly

Square
spot

Did you
know?

A seven-spot ladybug
can eat up to 30 greenfly
or blackfly in 60 minutes.
That's one fly every
two minutes!

Bees and wasps

Bees and wasps are insects. They feed on sweet nectar from flowers. Wasps can be troublesome in summer when they buzz around sugary foods.

◄ A beehive has six-sided cells where the eggs and grubs live, and where bees store honey.

◄ Wasps feed their grubs inside the small cells where they hatch from eggs.

Spotting bees and wasps

🐝 Each hive, or nest, is home to a large number of bees or wasps and their mother— the **queen**.

🐝 **Pollen** from flowers gets stuck on the bees' hairy coat. The pollen is passed by accident from one flower to another by bees. This **pollinates** the flowers.

🐝 For most of summer, wasps catch and kill insects, which they feed to their grubs.

Did you know?

Honeybees are good at finding flowers and remembering where they are. When they get back to the hive they do a special dance, which may help to tell the other **worker** bees where to go.

Do I have a fat, hairy body? Am I mainly black with gold, red, or white markings?

Do I have a black body with yellow stripes and black spots?

Black spot

Fat, hairy body

Yellow stripe

Common wasp

Length: 0.8 in (22 mm)
Food: Mostly insects. Ripe fruit and sweet foods in late summer
Habitat: Almost everywhere in the town and countryside
Eggs: Laid by the queen wasp inside the nest

Bumble bee

Length: 0.7 in (18 mm)
Food: Pollen and nectar from flowers
Habitat: Backyards, parks, farmland, woodland
Eggs: Laid by queen bumble bee inside the nest

Honeybee

Length: 0.6 in (16 mm)
Food: Pollen and nectar from flowers
Habitat: Almost anywhere where there are flowers
Eggs: Laid by the queen bee inside the hive

Am I quite small and mainly black or brown? Do I have an orange band on my abdomen?

WARNING!

Don't get too close to bees or wasps. They can sting if they feel threatened or see sudden movement.

Orange band

Pollen

23

Ants

Ants live in large **colonies**, or groups. There may be 100,000 ants in a colony, but they all have the same mother—the queen ant. The ants that you see most often are the worker ants. These are female ants that are unable to lay eggs.

Watch it!

Look out for flying ants swarming in the air. These are the males and egg-laying females leaving the nest for their mating flight. After they have mated, the males die, but the females begin to make new nests to lay eggs in.

Am I small and dark brown or black all over?

Dark-brown body

Spotting ants

🐜 There are about 14,000 different kinds of ant in the world. Ants are insects. Most have a fat abdomen, long legs, and strong jaws.

🐜 The worker ants do not have wings because they live in sheltered nests where wings would get in the way.

🐜 Ants feed on many kinds of food, but most like sweet things. Some ants milk greenfly and blackfly for a sweet liquid, called **honeydew**, that they produce.

Black garden ant

Length: 0.2 in (5 mm) (worker ant)
Food: Plants, seeds, small animals, and honeydew
Habitat: Everywhere in the town and countryside
Eggs: Laid in an underground nest by the queen ant

Am I small and yellow-brown in color? Do I live in grassy areas?

Yellow meadow ant

Length: 0.1in (3 mm) (worker ant)

Food: Plants, seeds, and other small animals

Habitat: Grassland. Its nests look like mounds of sand or soil

Eggs: Laid underground by the queen ant

Am I small and yellow? Am I inside a house or warm building?

Yellow-brown abdomen

Wood ant

Length: About 0.2 in (6 mm) (worker ant)

Food: Plants, seeds, and small animals

Habitat: Woodland that has trees with needle-shaped leaves

Eggs: Laid by the queen ant in a huge nest made of tree leaves

Yellow body

Am I large with a red thorax and a dark-colored abdomen? Do I live in woodland?

Red thorax

Pharaoh's ant

Length: 0.1 in (2 mm) (worker ant)

Food: Scraps of human food

Habitat: In cracks inside warm buildings

Eggs: Laid by the queen in nests inside crevices, or cracks, in warm buildings

Spiders

Spiders feed mainly on insects, many of which are flies. Larger spiders that live in the tropics can catch and eat small birds and mice.

Am I brown in color with a white cross on my back?

White cross

Spotting spiders

 All spiders have eight legs and most have eight eyes. Their body has two parts to it—the cephalothorax, a combination of the head and thorax joined together, and the abdomen.

All spiders can make silk. The silk leaves the spider's body as a liquid, but it hardens as soon as it touches the air. Some spiders use silk to make traps, called webs, to catch their **prey**.

There are more than 40,000 different kinds of spider.

Garden spider

Length: About 0.5 in (13 mm)
Food: Small flying insects, which it traps in its web
Habitat: Backyards, parks, woodland, waste ground, and hedgerows
Eggs: Up to 800 eggs are laid on fence posts and in cracks in trees

Watch it!

Find a spider's web and gently break part of the web with the tip of a blade of grass. Look again the next morning. Has the spider mended its web?

Long leg

House spider

Length: 0.4 in (10 mm)
Food: Small insects, which it traps in its web
Habitat: In buildings
Eggs: Laid inside a wrapping of silk inside a building

Do I have very long legs? Is my body yellow or red—brown in color with patches on it?

Do I have long legs? Do I have a pale stripe down the middle of my cephalothorax?

Female with an egg sac

Am I small, and yellow or white in color? Do I have a fat body and legs that look like a crab's?

Legs like a crab

Pale stripe

Long leg

Crab spider

Length: 0.4 in (10 mm)
Food: Small insects, which it catches by surprise
Habitat: Among tall grasses and on flowers
Eggs: Females lay eggs in a bag of silk

Wolf spider

Length: 0.3 in (8 mm)
Food: Small insects, which it chases
Habitat: Bare ground in backyards, parks, farmland, and woodland
Eggs: Females lay their eggs in a silk ball

Many legs

All insects have six legs, while spiders have eight legs. Some small animals have many more legs than this. They include woodlice, centipedes, and millipedes. These animals can be found hiding in rotting wood, under stones, logs, or heaps of dead tree leaves.

?

Am I long? Do I have one pair of antennae? Am I made up of segments with two pairs of legs on each?

Two legs on each segment

Spotting bugs with many legs

🐝 A woodlouse has 14 legs and its body is covered with hard plates that overlap like the tiles of a roof.

🐝 Centipedes and millipedes are usually much longer than woodlice. Their bodies are made up of segments. Some can have several hundred legs.

🐝 Woodlice and millipedes mainly eat dead plants.

🐝 Centipedes feed on tiny animals such as insects and their grubs.

Millipede

Length: 0.8–2 in (20–50 mm)
Food: Dead plants and rotting wood
Habitat: Under logs, stones, bark, and dead leaves
Eggs: Some millipedes lay their eggs in tiny nests

**Am I long?
Do I have one
pair of antennae?
Am I made up of
segments with
only one pair
of legs on
each segment?**

Centipede

Length: 1–3 in (25–80 mm)
Food: Small animals such as insects
and their grubs
Habitat: Under logs, stones, bark,
and heaps of dead leaves
Eggs: The female rolls her eggs along
the ground so that they look like
lumps of soil

Long
antenna

**Am I mainly gray or
dark brown in color?
Do I sometimes roll up
into a tight ball?**

**Am I mainly
gray or dark
brown in color?
Do I have 14 legs
and a pair of
long antennae?**

Pill woodlouse

Length: 0.7 in (18 mm)
Food: Dead plants, rotting wood
Habitat: In damp places, such as
under tree bark, logs and
stones, and under heaps of
rotting leaves
Eggs: Laid in the mother's pouch

Gray
body

Rolled
up

Woodlouse

Length: 0.7 in (18 mm)
Food: Dead plants, rotting wood
Habitat: In damp places, such as
under tree bark, logs and stones,
and under heaps of rotting leaves
Eggs: Laid in the mother's pouch

Antenna

Did you know?

In Central and South
America, centipedes can
grow up to 12 inches
(30 centimeters) long.
They can give people
painful bites.

Look, no legs!

Some animals, such as slugs and snails, have a "foot." The foot is the underside of their body. It is made of tiny muscles that help them to move. Snails are better protected than slugs because they have a shell to help them hide from their enemies or bad weather.

Is my shell large and rounded? Is it mainly light brown in color and patterned with darker bands?

Large shell

Spotting slugs and snails

- The shell of a snail is made of a chalky material produced by the snail's body. A snail can pull its whole body into the shell, but it can never leave the shell altogether.

- Slugs look like snails without shells, although some slugs have a small shell that is hidden under the skin.

- Both slugs and snails have two pairs of tentacles on their heads. The larger pair has eyes on their tips. The smaller pair of tentacles is used for smelling.

Garden snail

Shell size: Up to 1.5 in (38 mm) high and 1.3 in (35 mm) wide

Food: Living and dead plants, such as cabbages and lettuces

Habitat: Almost anywhere there are plants growing, especially in backyards and parks

Eggs: Laid in groups in damp soil

Am I large and completely black? Do I sometimes curl up?

Black body

Great black slug

Length: Up to 6 in (15 cm)
Food: Plants, droppings
Habitat: Parks, woodland, backyards, and waste ground
Eggs: Laid in clusters in damp soil or compost heaps

Is my shell tiny and almost see-through? Is it cone shaped with a blunt tip?

Cone-shaped shell

Moss snail

Shell size: Up to 0.2 in (6 mm) long and 0.1 in (3 mm wide)
Food: Small plants
Habitat: Almost everywhere that is damp, including under dead leaves, logs, and in long grass
Eggs: Laid in clusters in damp soil or mossy plants

Am I small and very slimy? Am I gray, light brown, or pale yellow in color?

Slimy body

Netted slug or field slug

Length: Up to 1 in (2.5 cm)
Food: Mainly green plants
Habitat: Backyards, parks, and farmland
Eggs: Laid in clusters in damp soil or under stones

Watch it!

Line an old margarine container with damp paper towels and make air-holes in the lid. Put a snail in it and surround it with different kinds of food such as a piece of apple and potato. Which foods does the snail like best?

The earthworm

Although they are usually small, earthworms are some of the most important animals in the world. Luckily, there are millions of them. An area the size of a soccer field could be home to five million worms.

Am I long and thin, with no legs, eyes, or ears? Am I made up of segments with a fatter area, called the saddle, toward the front end?

Segment

Saddle

Mouth

Spotting the earthworm

🐛 An earthworm has a head and a tail, but most of its body is made up of segments that are very similar to each other. Each of these segments has a number of small, stiff hairs on it. These help the worm to grip the sides of the burrow that it lives in.

🐛 Worms have no ears, eyes, or nose. Their skin is sensitive to light.

🐛 Worms are very good for soil because their burrows allow air and water to reach plant roots. Their wormcasts, or droppings, help to make the soil more **fertile**.

Earthworm
Length: 1–7 in (3–18 cm)
Food: Dead leaves, decaying plants, and animal material
Habitat: In soil
Eggs: Laid in a little brown bag, or cocoon, about 0.2 in (6 mm) long

Dead tree leaves

← Wormcasts show where earthworms have been feeding during the night.

Earthworm

Colored soil

Make a wormery

You will need:
- Large, see-through jar
- Small amounts of three different-colored soils
- Piece of cling wrap
- Small amount of sand or chalk
- Sheet of black paper
- Sticky tape
- Dead tree leaves
- Three earthworms

1. Remove any stones or lumps from the soils and put layers of each colored soil in the jar.
2. Next, put a thin layer of sand or chalk on the soils. Add some water to keep the soils moist.
3. Put in the earthworms and lay the dead leaves on the surface.
4. Cover the outside of the jar with black paper. Keep the wormery in a cool, dark place.
5. After a few days, remove the black cover to see what has happened. Record the results.
6. Return the worms to where you found them.

Bugs in danger

Although bugs seem to be everywhere, many kinds are in danger of dying out altogether. This is called **extinction**. Most are facing extinction because of things that humans do.

Habitat loss

Every kind of bug lives in particular surroundings. This is its habitat, or home. All over the world, humans are destroying habitats. Marshes and wetlands are being drained, and woods and forests are being cleared to provide land for roads and factories. In many other places, soil that bugs live in is being covered over with concrete and buildings.

⬆ This land is being cleared to make way for a new road. The bugs that live and lay eggs here will have to find somewhere else to go.

⬇ Collections of rare butterflies and moths were once sold for a lot of money.

Collecting

In some parts of the world, many large butterflies and moths are collected and killed. They are then used to make pictures, or other ornaments, for tourists to buy as souvenirs.

The chemical being sprayed on this field may kill the useful bugs as well as the harmful ones.

Pollution

Many bugs have been killed by **pollution**, such as chemicals used on farms to kill pests or to make crops grow better. Often, these chemicals kill useful animals, such as ladybugs and bees, as well as the pests. If the chemicals do not kill the bugs, they may kill the plants that the bugs need for food or to lay their eggs on.

Did you know?

More than 1,000 different kinds of butterfly are in danger of becoming extinct. In many parts of the world, colonies of honeybees are dying out.

Watch it!

Everyone can help bugs by making the areas around homes and schools safe for them to lay eggs and feed. Even if you don't have a backyard, you can plant pots, tubs, or window boxes with the flowers that bees, butterflies, and other insects like to visit.

If you find a bug somewhere where it might get hurt, move it carefully to a safe place.

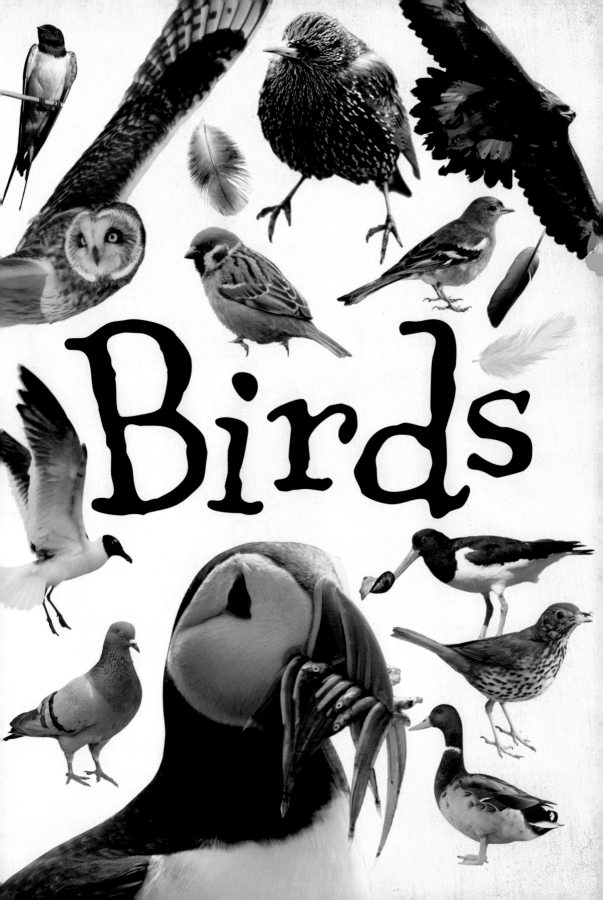

Birds

What is a bird?

Birds are the only animals that have feathers. A bony **skeleton** supports their body. They lay eggs with a hard shell. Most birds build **nests** to keep their eggs and young safe and sheltered. Birds can live all over the world.

Scrape

Hole nest

Nests

Nests come in many shapes and sizes. Most nests are cup shaped and are built in trees and bushes, but others are dome shaped. Some birds make nests on the ground or on beaches. This kind of nest is called a scrape. Some nests are built on the sides of buildings, or in holes in trees and are called hole nests. Nests are made of many materials, including sticks and mud.

➡ Ostriches are the largest birds in the world.

Did you know?

There are more than 9,000 different **species**, or kinds, of bird. The largest bird is the ostrich. It can grow up to 8 feet (2.5 meters) in height, and its eggs can weigh up to 4 pounds (1.8 kilograms).

Dome-shaped nest

Cup-shaped nest

Legs, wings, and beaks

All birds have wings, but some birds, such as penguins, cannot fly. A bird's legs are covered in **scales**. Scales are flat, hard pieces of skin that overlap each other. Birds have hard beaks, but their mouths are soft inside, like a human's. Birds use their beaks to pick up things and clean themselves.

Flight feathers

⬆ Although penguins cannot fly, they use their wings as paddles when they swim underwater.

Beak

➡ Doves are strong fliers. Their flight feathers push and steer them through the air.

Body feathers

Tail feathers

Scaly legs and clawed feet

Body feather

Down feather

Flight feather

Feathers

Feathers are made of the same material as a human hair and fingernails. There are three main types of feather. Down feathers grow close to the skin and help to keep the bird warm. Body feathers cover the bird like a waterproof jacket and give it a **streamlined** shape. Flight feathers on the wings and tail help the bird to fly.

Be a bird watcher

You can be a bird watcher whether you live in a town or city or in the countryside. You can even study the birds you see on your way to and from school.

Equipment

These are the main items you will need for birdwatching:

- Notebook
- Pen or pencil
- Binoculars to make the bird seem much nearer

⬇ Use binoculars to see birds more clearly when you go out birdwatching.

Binoculars

Did you know?

The vervain hummingbird of Jamaica lays the world's smallest egg. It is about the size of a small pea.

Identifying birds

You can identify different species of bird by looking at their shapes, colors, and markings. A backyard or park is a good place to start birdwatching. Once you have identified a bird, you could make a table in your notebook to record your findings.

↑ When you see a bird, draw a simple sketch in your notebook. You can add details about the bird's colors and markings.

Close-up with binoculars

Date	Type of bird	Time of day	Place	Kind of weather	What was the bird doing?	Was the bird alone?
March 2	Magpie	10 a.m.	The park	Sunny	Sitting in the trees	In a pair
April 28	Coot	3.30 p.m.	The river	Breezy	Swimming	Yes
July 18	Barn owl	7.30 p.m.	The woods	Warm	Flying	Yes

WARNING!

Always tell an adult when and where you are going birdwatching, and never leave the adult you are with without permission.

Carry a spare pen or pencil, just in case you need it

City birds

Some birds live in busy towns and cities. They often feed on the scraps of food that people put out for them. You can see these birds in the countryside as well.

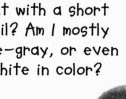

Am I quite fat with a short tail? Am I mostly blue-gray, or even white in color?

Small head

Rounded body

Spotting city birds

🌿 **Feral** pigeons often live in large numbers. They are seen on city buildings and in parks and backyards, often feeding on scraps of food.

🌿 Starlings can be seen in many places, walking on the ground as they look for insects and grubs. In summer, starlings often gather together in **flocks** of thousands.

🌿 Magpies are often seen in pairs, crowing, or calling, in the trees. Some people do not like them because they kill and eat baby birds. However, most of their food comes from animals that have been killed on the road.

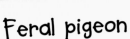

Feral pigeon

Length: 14 in (35 cm)
Habitat: Cities, towns, ruined buildings, farms
Food: Human food scraps, seeds, plants
Nest: On ledges on buildings
Eggs: 2, but breed all year round

Am I quite large with a short beak? Am I black and white? Do I have a long tail?

Long, green-black tail

White patch on wing

Blue-black wing

Yellow beak

Am I quite small? Do I have a thin beak and green or purple feathers with spots on?

Spotted breast

Magpie

Length: 20 in (50 cm)
Habitat: Parks, backyards, grassland with trees, farmland, woodland, by the sea
Food: Insects, slugs, worms, small birds, grains, fruit, dead animals, or **carrion**
Nest: Large domed nest of sticks in a tree or thorn bush
Eggs: 5-7

Starling

Length: 9 in (24 cm)
Habitat: Towns, cities, farmland, cliffs, woodland
Food: Insects, seeds, berries, fruit, grains, human food scraps
Nest: In holes in trees and buildings and under climbing plants
Eggs: 4-7

Watch it!

Which foods do birds like best? Choose some different foods, such as seeds and bread, and put each kind of food in a dish. Put the dishes outside. Which food is eaten first?

43

Small birds with short beaks

Many small birds have strong, short beaks. They use their beaks to crack open seeds. These birds will eat other foods, too, particularly in winter when they are hungry.

Am I quite small with a brown beak and a gray head?

Gray head

Pale eyebrow

Black bib

MALE

Am I small with a brown beak and a dull, gray underside?

Dull, gray underside

Spotting small birds with short beaks

- House sparrows live in flocks. The male has a small, black spot underneath its beak that looks like a baby's bib.

- In winter, tree sparrows sometimes join flocks of house sparrows and other small birds.

- The male chaffinch has a gray-blue top to his head and a pink chest. The female is duller in color.

House sparrow

Length: 6 in (15 cm)
Habitat: Houses, farms, parks, and backyards
Food: Human food scraps, seeds, insects
Nest: In holes, or in ivy or other thick plant growth
Eggs: 3–6

FEMALE

Brown head

Black cheek patch

Am I small with a brown top to my head? Do I have a black patch on my cheek?

Tree sparrow

Length: 6 in (15 cm)
Habitat: Old trees, ruined buildings, cliffs
Food: Seeds and insects
Nest: Mostly in holes in trees
Eggs: 4–6

Am I small with a white patch on my shoulder and a white stripe on my wings?

Gray-blue head

White stripe

Pink chest

White shoulder

MALE

Am I small with a white stripe on my wings?

Chaffinch

Length: 6 in (16 cm)
Habitat: Parks, backyards, woods, farmland in winter
Food: Seeds, fruit, insects
Nest: Small cup-shaped nest in bushes and trees
Eggs: 4–5

White stripe

WARNING!

If birds live near your home, don't go near their nest. The parent birds may leave the nest because they are scared, and never come back to their babies.

FEMALE

45

Small birds with thin beaks

Birds with short, thin beaks mainly use them for picking up insects and insect grubs. If they are really hungry, they will eat other foods, too, such as seeds and berries.

Am I very small and brown? Do I have a short, turned-up tail?

Turned-up tail

Brown coloring

Spotting small birds with thin beaks

- Wrens are small, active birds that move quickly on the ground like mice. Their song is very loud for such a tiny bird.

- Song thrushes crack open snail shells by beating them on a stone. They then use their beak to pull out the animal inside the shell before eating it.

- Long-tailed tits build an oval nest made of moss and lichens and lined with feathers. The nest has a hole in the side.

Wren

Length: 4 in (10 cm)
Habitat: Backyards, parks, woods, farmland, bushes, hedges, cliffs
Food: Insects, seeds
Nest: Domed nest in hedges or ivy, and in crevices, or cracks
Eggs: 5–8

Pink shoulders

Am I very small and light colored underneath? Do I have a long, narrow tail?

Long, narrow tail

Long-tailed tit

Length: 6 in (14 cm)
Habitat: Edges of woods and forests, thick hedges, parks
Food: Insects and seeds
Nest: Oval ball in a thorny bush or high up a tree
Eggs: 7-12

Do I have a brown back and a light-colored underside covered in dark spots?

Brown back

Spotted underside

Song thrush

Length: 9 in (24 cm)
Habitat: Backyards, parks, thick hedges, woods, bushes
Food: Snails, slugs, worms, insects, berries
Nest: Cup-shaped nest in hedges, trees, ivy and sheds
Eggs: 4-6

Watch it!

Make a bird bath using a shallow bowl. Sink the bowl into the ground before you fill it with clean water. Record which birds come to bathe or drink.

Birds with forked tails

Some birds have forked tails. Their tails separate into two points at the end, instead of being one whole section. As winter approaches, birds with forked tails fly to warmer countries. This is called **migration**.

White underside

Spotting birds with forked tails

- Swifts have weak legs, so they cannot walk on the ground. They take off from high places to jump straight into the air.
- House martins build nests under the **eaves** of buildings such as houses and barns, under bridges, and on cliffs.
- Swallows build nests in barns, on ledges, and in rafters. They sometimes hunt over water.

Short, forked tail

House martin

Length: 5 in (13 cm)
Habitat: Towns, villages, bridges, cliffs
Food: Flying insects
Nest: Nest made of mud, under house eaves and bridges, or on cliffs
Eggs: 4–5

Do I have long pointed wings? Do I look black all over except for a white patch under my throat?

Did you know?
A swift spends most of its life flying. It only lands to lay eggs and look after its young. At night, it sleeps while flying in the sky.

Long, narrow wing

Short, forked tail

White patch

Do I have long wings, a long, forked tail, and a red patch on my head?

Red patch

Swift

Length: 6 in (17 cm)
Habitat: Spends most of the time in the air, particularly over towns, cities, and water
Food: Flying insects
Nest: In holes in roofs and on ledges, church towers and cliffs
Eggs: 2–3

Long, forked tail

Swallow

Length: 6–8 in (16–22 cm)
Habitat: Farms, edges of towns and cities, villages
Food: Flying insects
Nest: Nest made of mud, on ledges in farm buildings, houses, sheds
Eggs: 4–6

Birds of prey

? Am I very large, with long wings and a rounded tail? Do I fly high in the sky and glide a long way?

Pale head and neck

Birds of prey hunt during the day. They have a hooked beak for tearing off flesh. They also have long, sharp claws, called **talons**, that they use to catch and hold their **prey**.

Dark-brown back

Spotting birds of prey

🦅 Golden eagles live in lonely places where there are few people around, such as on mountains or cliffs by the sea.

🦅 Kestrels hunt over farmland, meadows, parks, towns, moors, and marshes.

🦅 When hunting their prey, peregrine falcons are the fastest-flying birds in the world.

Large talon

Golden eagle

Length: 30–35 in (76–90 cm)
Habitat: Mountains, moorland, hills, cliffs, pine forests
Food: Small mammals, birds, carrion
Nest: Big pile of sticks and twigs on cliffs or in trees
Eggs: 2

Pointed wing

Long tail

Do I have a long tail, pointed wings, and a blue–gray head? Do I hover in the air?

?

?

Am I quite large with pointed wings? Is my tail thin at the end? Do I fly high in the sky?

Hooked beak

White face

Striped underside

Kestrel

Length: 14 in (36 cm)
Habitat: Farmland, open woods, parks, towns, cliffs, moorland, by highways
Food: Small mammals, birds, and insects
Nest: In old crows' nests, hollow trees, or on the ground
Eggs: 4–6

Peregrine falcon

Length: 19 in (48 cm)
Habitat: Mountains, moorland, cliffs by sea, cities, and over marshes in winter
Food: Mainly pigeons and other birds
Nest: Mostly on cliff ledges, but sometimes on tall city buildings and high bridges
Eggs: 2–6

Birds of the night

Am I a large brown and black owl with "ears" on the top of my head?

Ear tuft

Orange eye

Hooked beak

Most birds are active during the day and, like us, they sleep at night. However, there are a few birds that are **nocturnal**, or awake at night.

Talon

Spotting owls

🐾 Many owls are nocturnal. All owls have extremely good eyesight and hearing. Unlike most birds, owls have eyes that face forward.

🐾 Owls can turn their heads all the way around so that they can see behind them.

🐾 Many owls have feathers that match their surroundings, so they are hard to see when they are resting. This is called **camouflage**.

Long-eared owl

Length: 15 in (37 cm)
Habitat: Woods, forests, moors, marshes
Food: Small mammals, birds, insects
Nest: In old birds' or squirrels' nests, such as those of magpies, or on the ground
Eggs: 3–6

Am I light brown with a white face?

Watch it!

When owls eat small animals, they also swallow the bones and fur. The birds cough up these unwanted parts as a pellet. Wearing gloves, find an owl pellet, then soak it in water. Use tweezers to pull it apart and see what the owl ate.

Am I a large, gray-colored bird with long wings that have black stripes on them?

Short ear tufts

Yellow eye

Rounded head

White face

Pale, speckled chest

Black stripes

Barn owl

Length: 14 in (36 cm)
Habitat: Farmland, parks, open countryside
Food: Mainly rats, mice, and voles, but also small birds and insects
Nest: Old buildings, hollow trees
Eggs: 3–11

Short-eared owl

Length: 15 in (39 cm)
Habitat: Moors, marshes, grassy areas, sand dunes, countryside
Food: Small mammals, birds, insects
Nest: On the ground
Eggs: 4–7

Water birds

Many different kinds of bird live near water. Some of them can walk across water plants. Others dive under the water to catch food. Some have long legs so they can walk through water, while a few have long necks that help them reach water plants and animals underwater.

Am I quite large and mainly black in color? Do I have a white patch at the front of my head?

White patch

Lobed foot

Spotting water birds

🌱 Herons stand in shallow water looking for food. They nest high up in trees in groups called heronries.

🌱 Coots live on lakes and rivers in the town and countryside. They have strange lobed, or rounded, feet that help them to swim and dive.

🌱 Dippers feed by diving or walking underwater on the bottoms of streams and shallow rivers. They look for water insects and other small animals.

Coot

Length: 16 in (40 cm)
Habitat: Lakes, rivers, and reservoirs
Food: Mainly water plants, but also insects, water snails, tadpoles, and fish eggs
Nest: Built in reeds or rushes and resting on the water
Eggs: 4–8

Am I small and dark brown with a white throat and chest? Am I in or near a fast-flowing river or stream?

Sharp beak

Am I large and mainly gray in color? Do I have a very long neck, long legs, and a large, sharp beak?

White throat

Short tail

Long neck

Dipper

Length: 7 in (18 cm)
Habitat: Fast-flowing streams and rivers
Food: Water insects and other small animals
Nest: Domed nest on ledges or near water
Eggs: 4-6

Gray heron

Length: 40 in (100 cm)
Habitat: Rivers, lakes, marshes, estuaries
Food: Fish, frogs, voles, insects
Nest: Nests in a heronry in tall trees, sometimes far from water
Eggs: 3-5

Baby coot

Did you know?

Baby coots are black and fluffy with bright-red heads. They can swim as soon as they hatch.

Long legs

55

Ducks, geese, and swans

Am I very large with a black head, long, black neck and a white patch under my chin?

Ducks, geese, and swans are large birds that live on or near water. They mainly live near lakes, ponds, and rivers, but some also live near salt-water areas such as the sea.

White patch

Black head

Brown back

Spotting ducks, geese, and swans

Mallards are the most common ducks in the city and countryside.

Canada geese are often seen in large, noisy flocks. The goslings, or babies, are green-yellow or brown in color.

Swans have huge wings, and when they fly they make a swishing sound.

Canada goose

Length: 35–45 in (90–110 cm)
Habitat: Lakes, rivers, marshes, and farmland
Food: Grass, water plants
Nest: Made of weeds
Eggs: 5–7

Do I have a shiny green head and a black tail?

Green head

Curly tail feather

Am I brown with a yellow beak?

FEMALE

MALE

Yellow beak

Mallard

Length: 24 in (62 cm)
Habitat: Any fresh or salt water
Food: Seeds, plants, small animals
Nest: In sheltered spots on the ground or in holes in trees
Eggs: 9–12

Am I very large and white in color? Do I have a long neck and an orange beak?

Orange beak

Long, curved neck

Mute swan

Length: 63 in (160 cm)
Habitat: Any fresh or salt water, including lakes, rivers, marshes, bays, estuaries
Food: Water plants and grass
Nest: On banks, in marshes, or among reeds
Eggs: 2–9

Did you know?

Mute swans can live for more than 20 years.

57

Seabirds

The sea can be a difficult place for a bird to live. Storms, winds, and huge waves are very dangerous. Some seabirds spend their lives out at sea, only coming on land to lay their eggs.

Am I quite large and mostly white, with a dark-brown head and a dark-red beak and legs?

Dark-brown head

Dark-red legs

Red beak

Spotting seabirds

Black-headed gulls are one of many kinds of gull. In winter they come inland and their heads become mainly white.

The oystercatcher is common on the seashore where it can feed on shellfish, small crabs, and other small creatures that live in the mud or sand.

Puffins nest in colonies. They either dig their burrows themselves, or take over rabbits' burrows.

Black-headed gull

Length: 15 in (38 cm)
Habitat: By the sea, rivers and lakes, on farmland, and in city parks
Food: Small sea and land animals, seeds, scraps
Nest: Mostly in long grass by water
Eggs: 2–3

Am I mostly black and white with orange feet? Do I have a huge red, yellow, and blue beak?

Large, triangular beak

White face

Am I quite large and mostly black and white? Do I have pink legs and a long, orange beak?

Puffin

Length: 12 in (31 cm)
Habitat: By the sea and on cliffs
Food: Fish and small sea animals
Nest: In a colony of burrows on cliffs by the sea
Eggs: 1

Orange leg and foot

Long, orange beak

Pink leg

Oystercatcher

Length: 17 in (45 cm)
Habitat: Mainly on sandy and muddy shores
Food: Small animals living in sand, mud, and soil
Nest: A scrape on sand or in grass
Eggs: 2–4

Watch it!

If you see a bird's footprints by the seashore, take a photograph of them. You can look in a field guide to see which bird they belong to.

59

Woodland birds

Many birds live in woods and forests. They adapted, or changed, a long time ago to live in these places. Birds that climb trees have toes that allow them to cling to tree trunks. Birds that live on the ground are camouflaged among the grass and leaves.

Spotting woodland birds

- Woodcocks use their beaks to search for food. They stick them into soft ground to search for insects and other bugs.
- Although crossbills will eat other seeds, they mainly eat the seeds inside cones.
- Treecreepers have large claws and a long tail. Their slightly curved beak helps them to find insects and grubs in tree bark.

Am I a red—brown color all over with broad, dark stripes on the back of my head?

Woodcock

Length: 14 in (36 cm)
Habitat: Woodland and forest clearings with damp areas
Food: Worms, insects, spiders, centipedes
Nest: A leaf—lined scrape on the ground, under brambles or ferns
Eggs: 4

Dark stripes

Long beak

Red—brown feathers

Short leg

Watch it!

Fill a string bag (like those grocery stores sell onions in) with dried grass. Hang the bag from a tree. Push sticks into the bag to act as perches. Which birds come to your bag for nesting materials?

Am I small and brown with a long tail? Do I creep up tree trunks?

Treecreeper

Length: 5 in (13 cm)
Habitat: Woods, parks, and backyards
Food: Insects, small bugs
Nest: Behind tree bark or ivy, or in cracks in tree trunks
Eggs: 5–6

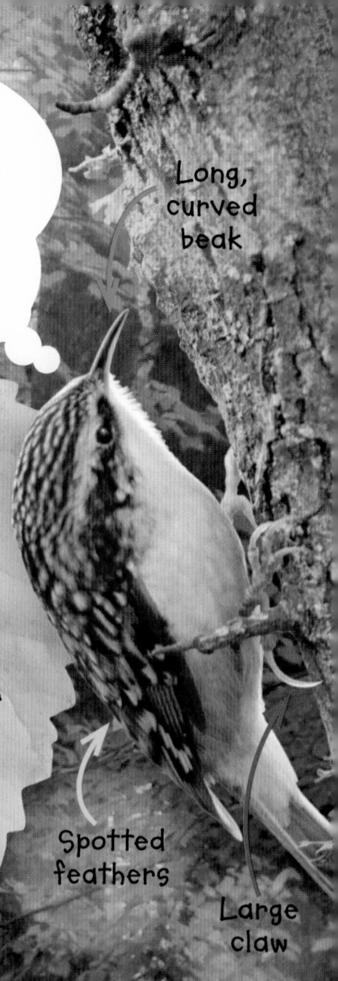

Long, curved beak
Spotted feathers
Large claw

Am I high up in trees that have cones? Am I mostly red? Do I have a beak where the two tips overlap?

Am I small and green in color? Do the tips of my beak overlap?

rossed beak
MALE
FEMALE
Green feathers

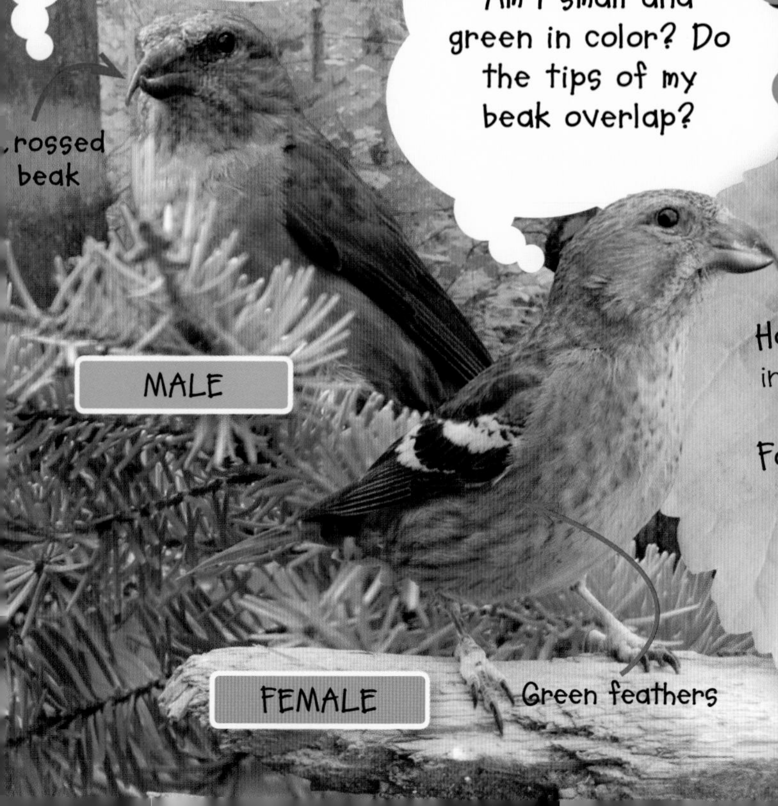

Crossbill

Length: 6 in (17 cm)
Habitat: Conifers, especially in woods and forests, but also in parks and backyards
Food: Conifer seeds, but also berries, thistle seeds, and insects
Nest: Cup-shaped nest high in conifers
Eggs: 3–4

Birds in danger

Many kinds of bird are in danger of dying out altogether. This is called **extinction**. Most of these birds are facing extinction because of things that human beings do.

Habitat loss

All over the world, people are destroying **habitats**, or places where birds live. Woods and forests are being cleared to provide land for farms, roads, houses, and factories. When these places are destroyed, the birds that lived there have nowhere to feed or breed.

⬆ When forests are cut down, the birds that live and breed there have to find somewhere else to go.

➡ In the future, some birds will not be able to live in the places where they do now. This is because of the effects of **pollution** on the Earth.

Hunting and collecting

In some parts of the world, many birds are killed for their meat, for their beautiful feathers, or just for fun. Some people collect wild birds to keep as pets, while other people make collections of birds' eggs.

← These parrots have been captured for their feathers or to be kept as pets.

Pollution

Many birds have been killed by chemicals used on farms to kill pests or to make crops grow better. At sea, oil spilled from ships kills thousands of birds every year. Litter can be harmful to wildlife. Plastic rings from packs of drinks can sometimes choke birds.

→ This oil-soaked penguin has been rescued. If its feathers can be cleaned, it may survive.

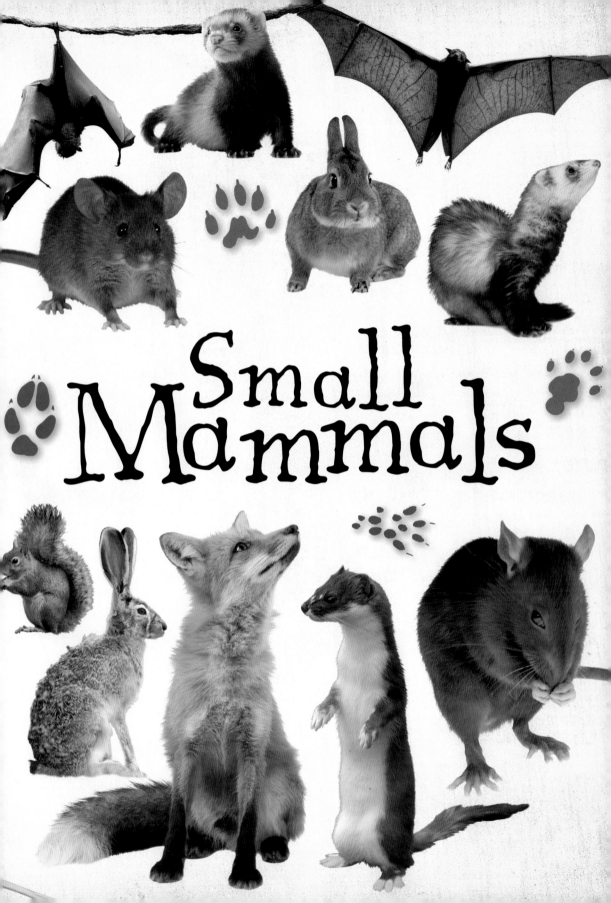

Small Mammals

What is a mammal?

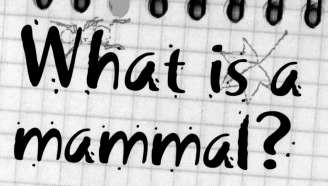

Mammals are the only animals with hair or fur. They feed their young on milk. Mammals live almost everywhere, from the hot tropics to the icy seas. The sort of place a particular mammal lives is called its **habitat**.

← A polar bear's thick, fleecy coat protects it from the icy cold winds in its Arctic home.

↓ Blue whales are the same length as 3.5 buses!

All shapes and sizes

Mammals come in many shapes and sizes, but they all have lungs and breathe air. They also have a skeleton with a backbone inside their body.

← A fox has good hearing and a keen sense of smell.

↑ These young rabbits are sitting outside the entrance to their **burrow**.

Senses

Like all animals, mammals spend their time finding food, keeping warm or cool, avoiding danger, finding a mate, and having babies. To help them do these things, mammals have well-developed senses for sight, hearing, smell, taste, and touch.

Young mammals

Most mammals give birth to several babies at the same time. They are called a **litter**. Some mammals make a nest for their young. Some burrow underground and make a **den**.

Did you know?

Blue whales are the largest animals in the world. They can grow up to 100 feet (30 meters) long and weigh more than 160 tons.

Length = 3.5 buses

Be a mammal watcher

Many mammals are **nocturnal**, or only active at night. They are very nervous of people. To see them, you have to search for clues about where they live.

→ These tracks in mud show that a fox has walked this way recently.

Sit quietly

Another good way to see mammals is just to sit quietly and wait. Choose a good spot where you think mammals may appear. You could look for their footprints in mud, soft ground or snow, or even for their droppings.

Know their habits

To watch a mammal, you have to know something about its habits—whether it is active by day or night, where it lives, and what it eats. If you spot a mammal, walk slowly and stop frequently to check whether it has noticed you. Make sure you stay at a safe distance from the mammal.

Footprint focus

Some mammals are only active at night, which makes it difficult to spot them. Looking for footprints is a good alternative—you can even make plaster casts of them. Find out how on page 73.

1.5 in (37 mm) wide

Keep a mammal diary

These are the main tools you will need to be a mammal watcher:
- Binoculars to see mammals from far away
- Pen
- Notebook to keep a mammal diary

➡ If you see a mammal you do not recognize, make a sketch in your notebook.

Date	Time and place	Mammal	Kind of weather	What was the mammal doing?	Was the mammal alone?
March 2	9.10 a.m. field of corn	Hare	Cold and windy	Boxing and chasing	With another hare
October 3	8.20 a.m. the park	Gray squirrel	Warm and sunny	Collecting acorns and burying them in the grass	Yes

WARNING!

Make sure you do not go out alone at night to watch mammals.

◀ Fresh droppings, such as these of a deer, show that the animal has passed this way.

Did you know?

There are more than 5,000 different **species** of mammal in the world, but mammals make up only 0.3 percent of all animal species. Most species of animal are insects.

The red fox

Foxes live in all sorts of places, from towns and cities to the countryside. Foxes have very good hearing and a strong sense of smell. Although they can see movement, they cannot see still objects very well.

> Do I look a bit like a dog? Am I a red–brown color? Do I have a bushy tail with a white tip?

Red–brown fur

2 in (60 mm) wide

Spotting foxes

- You can often tell where a fox has been because it leaves a musty smell, like stale food.

- If you find a hole about 10 inches (25 centimeters) high and 8 inches (20 centimeters) across with bones and feathers near the entrance, it may be a fox's den.

- A fox's footprints are about the size of an average dog's.

⬇ Fox cubs leave the den for the first time when they are about four weeks old.

Family life

Although you normally see a fox by itself, it lives in a family group. There is usually a dog fox (male), the vixen (female), and her cubs, or babies. They live in a den when they are breeding. This may be in a crack in a rock or under tree roots. Sometimes the vixen digs her own den, or she may live in an old burrow made by another animal. In cities, foxes may even make their den under a pile of garbage.

⬅ Fox cubs are taught how to stalk their prey and survive in the world by their parents.

Red fox
Head and body length: 26 in (66 cm)
Length of tail: 15 in (38 cm)
Habitat: Woodland, parks, farmland, towns, and cities
Activity: By day and night
Food: Small mammals, birds, insects, fruits, waste food from trash cans in cities
Young: 4–5 cubs in one litter each year

White tip

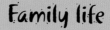

Did you know?

At night, you may hear foxes barking at each other, or calling for a mate.

Cats

Cats can be seen almost everywhere. Most of these cats are pets. However some cats live in the wild, too.

> Am I mostly ginger or black and white? Do I have large eyes at the front of my head and a pointed tip to my tail?

Large eye

1 in (30 mm) wide

Feral cat

Head and body length: About 19 in (50 cm)

Length of tail: About 12 in (30 cm)

Habitat: Countryside, in towns and cities

Activity: By day and night

Food: Small mammals and birds in the countryside. In towns and cities, waste food from trash cans

Young: About 3 kittens in each of 3–4 litters every year

Spotting feral cats

- ❁ A **feral** cat is a pet cat that now lives in the wild. It could have been an unwanted pet, or a pet that got lost.
- ❁ Feral cats sometimes live in **colonies**, or groups, with other cats.

Pet footprints

As well as making plaster casts of the footprints of wild animals, you could make a cast of the footprints of your cat. Fill a shallow tray with soil or sand and smooth the surface so that it is flat. Stand the tray outside and encourage your cat to stand in it. When you have a clear footprint, make a plaster cast.

Make a plaster cast of animal footprints

You will need:

- Some plaster of Paris powder
- Strips of thin cardstock about 12 in (30 cm) long and 2 in (5 cm) wide
- Paperclips
- Container for mixing
- Small bottle of water
- Trowel
- Old spoon
- Paint and paintbrushes

1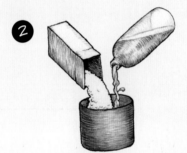

When you have found a clear footprint, circle it with the strip of cardstock. Push the cardstock a little way into the mud or sand and then hold the ends in place with a paperclip.

2

Put a small amount of water into the container and add the plaster of Paris powder, a little at a time, using a spoon. Keep stirring until the mixture is like thick cream.

3

Gently pour the liquid plaster inside the wall of cardstock until it is about 2 in (5 cm) deep. Tap the sides carefully to get rid of any air bubbles. Add some more plaster mixture if necessary.

4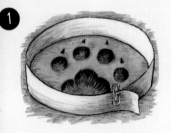

Leave the plaster for 30–60 minutes to set. Carefully dig it up with a trowel and take it home. Clean and paint the footprint.

Water mammals

Mink live mainly by rivers and lakes. Otters live by lakes, rivers, streams, and some coasts. Both mammals are nocturnal and good swimmers. They are **streamlined** so they can move quickly in water.

Am I dark in color? Do I have a pointed nose?

Pointed nose

Chocolate-brown fur

1 in (25 mm) wide

Spotting mink

- 🐾 A lot of mink live in North America. Some were brought to Europe in the late 1920s to be kept for their fur. Many escaped and began to breed in the wild.

- 🐾 Mink eat fish, birds, and small mammals, and will even raid fish farms for food.

Mink

Head and body length: 16 in (40 cm)
Length of tail: 5 in (12 cm)
Habitat: Lakes and rivers
Activity: At night
Food: Fish, water birds, small mammals
Young: 5-6 young in one litter each year

Do I have a wide flat head? Am I brown with a white throat? Can you only see my head above the water when I am swimming?

Spotting otters

🐾 Otters have small ears, a long body and a powerful tail. Their short, strong legs have webbed feet.

🐾 Otters are very playful. They sometimes chase each other and pretend to fight.

🐾 Otters build their holts, or dens, near water. They are lined with reeds, grass, and moss.

Thick, tapered tail

2 in (55 mm) wide

Otter

Head and body length: 25–35 in (65–90 cm)
Length of tail: 16 in (40 cm)
Habitat: Near lakes, rivers, streams and marshes, some coasts
Activity: At night
Food: Mostly fish, but some frogs, toads and newts, birds, insects, and small mammals
Young: 2–3 cubs in a litter each year

Webbed feet

Weasels and stoats

Both weasels and stoats will kill and eat animals larger than themselves. They have long, thin bodies on short legs. They can often be seen in the daytime.

Weasel

Head and body length: 8 in (20 cm)
Length of tail: 2 in (5 cm)
Habitat: Woodland, mountains, sand dunes, and grassland
Activity: By day and night
Food: Mice and voles, rabbits, rats, birds, and insects
Young: 5–6 young in each of 1–2 litters every year

Spotting weasels

- Weasels are fierce hunters. They eat hundreds of mice in a year.
- Each weasel's hunting area is about the size of 3.5 to seven soccer fields.
- Like stoats, weasels often stand on their back legs to look around.
- In cold climates, weasels turn white in winter.

Do I have a long, thin body? Is my fur brown with a white underside? Is my tail short and brown?

0.5 in (12 mm) wide

Short, brown tail

Brown throat patch

Did you know?

Even when a stoat turns fully white, it still has a black tip to its tail.

➡ White stoats are camouflaged against the snow in winter.

? Do I have a long, slim body with a brown and back head? Is my underside white and does my tail have a black tip?

Creamy-white underside

Spotting stoats

🐾 The stoat's hunting ground usually covers about the size of 18 soccer fields.

🐾 Stoats can move very fast, reaching speeds of up to 20 miles (32 kilometers) an hour.

🐾 In colder parts of the world, stoats turn white in winter. They are then called ermine.

Stoat

Head and body length: 10 in (25 cm)
Length of tail: 3 in (7.5 cm)
Habitat: Woods, mountains, sand dunes, and grassland
Activity: By day and night
Food: Small mammals and large insects
Young: 6 or more babies in one litter every year

0.9 in (22 mm) wide

Rabbits and hares

Rabbits and hares have long ears, long back legs, and an extra pair of teeth in the front of their top jaw. They eat plants and rely on speed to outrun their enemies.

Do I run fast using my long back legs? Do my ears have black tips?

Black-tipped ear

1 in (30 mm) wide

Large, staring eye

Spotting hares

- If a hare is frightened, it can run at a speed of about 35 miles (56 kilometers) an hour.

- Hares do not dig a burrow. Their young, called leverets, are born in open nests.

Brown hare

Head and body length: 17–30 in (44–76 cm)
Length of tail: 4 in (11 cm)
Habitat: Open countryside, farmland, woodland, and mountain areas
Activity: At dusk and night
Food: Plants, fruit, bark, and twigs
Young: 2–3 young in 3 litters every year

Watch it!

Look out for rabbit droppings. They are small, round, and dry. Rabbits eat their own droppings to make sure they get all the goodness from their food.

Spotting rabbits

- 🐾 Rabbits live in groups in a system of burrows called a warren.

- 🐾 Rabbits can breed very quickly. In one year, a female rabbit can produce more than 20 young.

- 🐾 Rabbits rarely move more than about 460 feet (140 meters) from home. They eat away all the plants around their home, which gives a clear area to show up approaching enemies.

- 🐾 Rabbits have a good sense of smell and hearing.

Am I mainly gray or brown? Do I have a short tail that is white underneath?

Orange back of neck

Short tail

Rabbit

Head and body length: 20 in (48 cm)
Length of tail: 3 in (7 cm)
Habitat: Short grass or fields
Activity: At dawn, dusk, and night
Food: A wide range of plants, including farm and garden crops
Young: Up to 7 young in each of 3–5 litters every year

10 in (22 mm) wide

Squirrels

Squirrels are among the most common wild mammals in the town and countryside. They are easily recognized by their bushy tails.

Am I mainly gray or yellow-brown? Do I have a bushy tail?

I in (25 mm) wide

Sharp claws

Bushy tail

Spotting gray squirrels

🐾 The natural home of gray squirrels is eastern North America. Gray squirrels were introduced into Europe in the 19th century.

🐾 Gray squirrels have few natural enemies in Europe. They have spread almost everywhere, including parks and backyards.

Gray squirrel
Head and body length: 12 in (30 cm)
Length of tail: 9 in (23 cm)
Habitat: Trees, hedgerows, parks and backyards in towns and cities
Activity: By day
Food: Mainly nuts and seeds, also insects and birds' eggs
Young: Up to 7 young in each of 2 litters every year

Spotting red squirrels

- Until the arrival of gray squirrels, the only squirrels in Europe were red squirrels.

- Red squirrels are a red or chestnut color with a tail that is much bushier than that of the gray squirrel.

- Red squirrels are most likely to be seen in forests of pine, spruce, or larch trees.

Am I a red or chestnut color with a white underside? Is my bushy tail red–brown? Do I have ear tufts?

1 in (25 mm) wide

Ear tufts

Watch it!

Look out for pine cones that have been chewed by squirrels. Usually only the center of the cone is left. Hazelnuts eaten by squirrels are usually split into two halves. Gray squirrels often use a tree stump as a table.

Red squirrel

Head and body length: 8 in (20 cm)
Length of tail: 7 in (18 cm)
Habitat: Forests
Activity: By day
Food: Mainly conifer cones, fruits, and nuts
Young: 1–7 babies in 2 litters every year

Bushy tail

Chewed pine cone

Brown rats and house mice

Do I have gray-brown fur and small, hairy ears? Is my tail thick and scaly?

Gray-brown fur

Thick, scaly tail

Mice and rats can be found almost anywhere in the world. The brown or common rat and house mouse are known as pests.

1 in (25 mm) wide

Spotting brown rats

- Rats often live on farms, on garbage dumps, or along muddy shores where food is washed up by the tides.

- Many brown rats live in sewers. Here, they are likely to catch diseases, which they may spread.

- A female rat can have up to 50 young each year.

Brown rat

Head and body length: Up to 11 in (28 cm)
Length of tail: 9 in (23 cm)
Habitat: Buildings, sewers, on garbage dumps, and on farms
Activity: At night
Food: Almost anything, including stored human and animal food
Young: Up to 11 young in each of 5 litters every year

Greasy fur

Do I have large ears, a pointed nose, and a long, scaly tail? Is my gray-brown fur greasy?

0.4 in (10 mm) wide

Pointed nose

House mouse

Head and body length: About 3 in (8 cm)
Length of tail: About 3 in (8 cm)
Habitat: Buildings in winter, in hedgerows and on farmland in summer
Activity: At night
Food: Grass, plants, insects, human food
Young: 5–10 litters a year with 5–6 young in each litter

WARNING!

Do not touch wild rats and mice or anything that they may have touched.

Spotting house mice

🐾 House mice have a strong, musty, or stale, smell and greasy fur.

🐾 Mice are often found near food stores. They often spoil the food with their urine and droppings.

🐾 In summer, house mice may live in fields and hedgerows. Most of them spend the winter in buildings.

Did you know?

Although brown rats only weigh 25 ounces (700 grams), three of them can eat as much food as one adult human being.

Mice and voles

Wood, or deer, mice and voles live in wooded and grassy areas. They have many **predators** so the only way they can survive is by producing large numbers of young.

Spotting mice and voles

- 🐾 A wood mouse has large back feet, which allow it to leap like a tiny kangaroo.

- 🐾 Although it is small, a field vole is very aggressive. It makes loud squeaks and chattering noises to frighten other field voles away from its territory.

- 🐾 Each bank vole stays very near its nest. It usually goes no more than 165 feet (50 meters) away.

Do I have gray–brown fur and a very short tail? Do I have a blunt nose?

Blunt nose

Long whiskers

0.4 in (10 mm) wide

Field vole

Head and body length: About 4 in (10 cm)

Length of tail: About 1.5 in (4 cm)

Habitat: Mainly overgrown fields and rough grassland

Activity: By day and night

Food: Mainly grasses

Young: 4–6 young in each of 4–5 litters every year

Am I small with a sandy-brown coat? Are my eyes and ears large?

Large ear

Long tail

Wood or deer mouse

Head and body length: 3–5 in (8–13 cm)

Length of tail: 3–5 in (7–12 cm)

Habitat: Woodland, sand dunes, parks, and buildings

Activity: At night

Food: Mainly fruits, nuts, seeds, some snails, and insects

Young: 5 young in each of 4 litters every year

0.5 in (12 mm) wide

Do I have chestnut-red fur? Do I have small ears and a blunt nose?

Small ear

Chestnut-red fur

Bank vole

Head and body length: About 3.5 in (9 cm)

Length of tail: About 2 in (6 cm)

Habitat: Woodland, forest, and hedgerows

Activity: By day and night

Food: Fruits, nuts, seeds, flowers, and insects

Young: 4–5 young in each of 5 litters every year

0.3 in (8 mm) wide

Shrews and moles

Most small mammals spend quite a lot of time searching for food. Shrews and moles are some of the most active small mammals because they need to eat a lot.

Do I have a long, pointed nose and tiny eyes? Do I have short legs and a thin tail?

Spotting shrews

🐾 Most kinds of shrew need to eat their body weight in insects and worms each day.

🐾 Shrews have poor eyesight, but their sense of smell is very good. This helps them to find their food.

🐾 Shrews have special stink glands to defend themselves against larger animals. The smell stops animals such as cats and weasels from eating them.

Small, rounded ear

Long, pointed nose

0.3 in (7 mm) wide

Shrew

Head and body length: 3 in (8 cm)
Length of tail: 2 in (5 cm)
Habitat: Hedgerows, fields, woods, and parks
Activity: By day and night
Food: Earthworms, beetles, spiders, and other small animals
Young: Several litters each with 6–7 young every year

Find an area of grassland where moles have been busy making **molehills**. Which is the biggest molehill you can find? How far apart are the molehills?

Do I have short, black fur? Do I have tiny eyes and large, clawed front feet? Have I made a heap of soil on the surface of the ground?

Silky, black fur

Large claws

0.5 in (13 mm) wide

Spotting moles

- Moles spend most of their lives underground. They live and feed in long tunnels not more than three feet (one meter) below the surface.

- Some kinds of mole cannot see at all. This doesn't matter because underground it is dark all the time.

- Moles have powerful bodies and spade-like front paws, so they are very good at digging.

Mole

Head and body length:
3–7 in (7–18 cm)
Length of tail: 1.5 in (4 cm)
Habitat: In the soil under fields, farmland, backyards, and woodland
Activity: By day and night
Food: Earthworms and insect grubs
Young: One litter of 3–4 young every year

Bats

Bats are the only mammals with wings. A bat's wings stretch from the tips of the bat's finger down to its feet and across its tail. Bats can live almost anywhere in the world.

Am I large with a red-brown head and body? Do I have a large claw sticking out the front of my wings?

Large, pointed ear

Spotting bats

- Colonies of the common pipistrelle bat can be very large, with more than 1,000 bats in a group.

- In warm places, little brown bats do not **hibernate** in winter. In cold places, they **migrate** hundreds of miles in autumn to warmer places where they can hibernate.

- The greater fruit bat has the largest wingspan of any bat.

- Most bats feed on insects, but some, such as vampire bats in South and Central America, take blood from large birds or mammals.

Large eye

Greater fruit bat

Head and body length: 16 in (40 cm)
Wingspan: 60 in (150 cm)
Habitat: Tropical forest and scrub in South and Southeast Asia
Activity: At night
Food: Fruit
Young: One every year

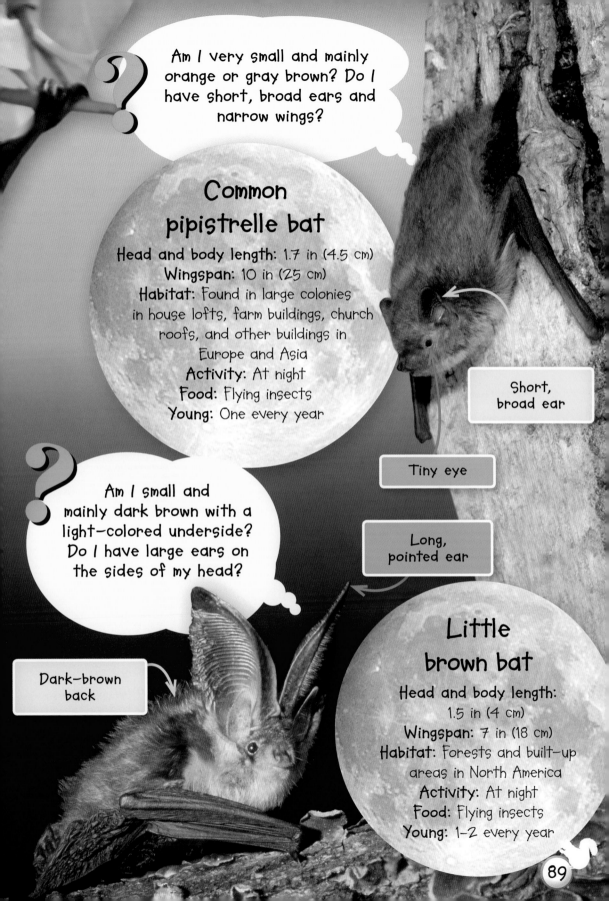

Am I very small and mainly orange or gray brown? Do I have short, broad ears and narrow wings?

Common pipistrelle bat

Head and body length: 1.7 in (4.5 cm)
Wingspan: 10 in (25 cm)
Habitat: Found in large colonies in house lofts, farm buildings, church roofs, and other buildings in Europe and Asia
Activity: At night
Food: Flying insects
Young: One every year

Short, broad ear

Tiny eye

Long, pointed ear

Am I small and mainly dark brown with a light-colored underside? Do I have large ears on the sides of my head?

Dark-brown back

Little brown bat

Head and body length: 1.5 in (4 cm)
Wingspan: 7 in (18 cm)
Habitat: Forests and built-up areas in North America
Activity: At night
Food: Flying insects
Young: 1–2 every year

Mammals in danger

About one-quarter of all species of mammal in the world are in danger of dying out altogether. This is called **extinction**. Most of these mammals are under threat, because of things that humans do. The three biggest threats to mammals are having their homes destroyed, being hunted, or being harmed by litter and other wastes.

▼ Red squirrels can live only where there are pine, fir, or spruce trees, with beech or oak trees nearby to provide them with food.

Habitat loss

One reason why there are fewer red squirrels is the loss of habitats such as woodland. When large areas of forest are cleared, red squirrels may have nowhere to go.

◀ There are only a few hundred mountain gorillas left in the world. Most of the forests where they live have been destroyed.

Hunting

In some parts of the world, many mammals are killed for their meat, fur, horns, or tusks, or just for fun. In some countries, mammals are killed so that parts of their bodies can be used as medicines.

➤ This oil-soaked otter has been rescued. If its fur can be cleaned, it may survive.

Watch it!

You can help wild mammals by not leaving litter that might damage their habitat or injure them. Mammals can get their heads trapped inside cans, drink cartons, or plastic cups when looking for food.

Pollution

Many mammals have been harmed by chemicals used on farms to kill pests and weeds. At sea, **pollution** such as oil spills from ships kills whales, dolphins, porpoises, and otters. Litter can be harmful to mammals and other wildlife. Broken bottles can cut mammals when they are looking for food.

Plants

What is a flower?

Most plants have flowers. They come in many shapes and sizes. Some smell like beautiful perfume, but a few smell horrible. All flowers have the same job. They make seeds so that new plants can grow.

Stigma — Style — STAMEN (male) — CARPEL (female)

Ovary

The parts of a flower

Most flowers have male and female parts. The male parts are called **stamens** and they produce tiny grains of yellow dust, called **pollen**. The female parts are called **carpels**. They are made up of a **stigma**, a **style**, and an **ovary**. The egg-cells are made in the ovaries. A new seed is made after a pollen grain joins with an egg-cell. This is called **fertilization**.

⬆ This lily flower has very large stamens and a large carpel in the middle of it.

Separate male and female plants

Not all plants have their male and female parts in the same flower. For example, there are separate male and female holly trees. Each tree has either male flowers or female flowers, but not both. Hazel trees have male and female flowers on the same tree.

Male holly flowers

Female holly flowers

Petals and sepals

There are other parts to most flowers, such as **petals**. Underneath the flower there are leaf-like parts called **sepals**.

Did you know?

The male flower of the birch tree is called a catkin. Each catkin can make more than five million pollen grains, which then blow away in the wind.

Petal

Sepal

Plant life

Many flowers are brightly colored to attract insects and other animals to them. These animals are important, because they carry pollen from one flower to another.

⬇ As this bee reaches into the flower to feed on nectar, pollen grains stick to its body.

Pollen

The importance of insects

A plant's egg-cells are usually fertilized by pollen from another plant of the same kind. Many flowers produce a sweet juice, called **nectar**, to attract animal pollen-carriers.

When an animal pushes into the flower to feed, pollen grains from the stamens stick to its body. On its visit to the next flower, some pollen may rub off onto the stigma. This is called **pollination**. A tiny tube grows down from the pollen grain into one of the egg-cells, and the egg-cell starts to grow into a seed. This is called fertilization.

Did you know?

Sometimes, the perfumes that flowers produce seem lovely to us. However, a few smell awful. The Rafflesia plant of Southeast Asia has the largest and smelliest flowers in the world.

↓ Catkins are the male flowers of hazel trees.

Going with the wind

Not all flowers are pollinated by insects or other animals. The wind spreads pollen between certain flowers, particularly those of grasses and many trees. These flowers are usually dull green and most do not have petals. They do not produce nectar or scent because they do not need to attract bees and other insects.

← These maple seeds have special "wings" that help them to move with the wind.

Be a plant spotter

Some parts of plants are small, so you need to get close to see all their details. One way is to collect them. Another way is to use a magnifying glass. The most important equipment you need is your eyes.

➡ **U**se plastic scissors to collect cuttings of plants.

The plant-spotter's collecting kit

Here is the equipment you will need to become a plant spotter:

- Magnifying glass to see all the details of the plant
- Plastic bags to store your finds until you get home
- Small envelopes for collecting seeds
- Sticky labels
- Plastic scissors
- Small paintbrushes and tweezers to pick up small parts of plants
- Plant pots (or clean yoghurt cups)
- Trowel
- Some soil or compost
- Notebook to record your findings
- Pen or pencil
- Crayons

⬆ **A** magnifying glass lets you see small things much more clearly.

WARNING!

It is against the law to collect wild seeds, plants, or flowers without permission from the owner of the land.

➡ **T**weezers are useful for picking up small parts of plants without damaging them.

➡ **When you see a flower, draw a sketch in your notebook. You can add details about the flower's colors.**

Keeping records

Every good plant spotter needs a notebook, some pencils, and colored crayons. Once you have found a flower, you could put the details in a table.

Date	Flower	Place	Where	Other flowers present	What was special about the flower?
January 3	Snowdrop	Westacre Park	In lawn, in sun	None	Growing through the snow
February 11	Hazel catkins	Wymbarton Wood	Woodland	Celandines	Pollen blowing away in the wind

Did you know?

There are more than 250,000 different **species**, or kinds, of flowering plant in the world.

Weed winners

A weed is a plant that grows where it is not wanted. Weeds can grow so quickly that they flower and produce new seeds before you have noticed them. Some weeds have bright, colorful flowers.

Is my flower large and red in color? Are my stamens black? Is my stem hairy?

Black stamens

Hairy stem

Spotting weeds

❀ Many weeds have a very short life cycle, from seeds to flowers and back to seeds again.

❀ Weeds produce a lot of seeds. Some of these seeds may stay hidden in the soil for many years until the conditions are right for them to grow.

❀ Some weeds have more than one way of surviving and spreading themselves. For example, if a dandelion plant is removed, some of its long root may stay in the soil. That piece of root will grow into a new plant.

Common or field poppy

Height: 8–23 in (20–60 cm)
Size of flower: 4 in (10 cm)
Flowers: Single flower on each stem
Habitat: Waste ground, roadsides, cornfields, and farmland
Fruits or seeds: Seeds inside a hard, round fruit
Flowering time: Early summer

Did you know?

Rosebay willowherb often grows on land that has been cleared by fire. It is also known as "fireweed."

Tall spike

Am I tall with no hairs? Are there a lot of purple flowers growing in a spike out of the top of me?

Bright-yellow flower

Is my flower bright yellow? Does my flower stem have several branches on it?

Meadow buttercup

Height: 12–40 in (30–100 cm)
Size of flower: 1 in (3 cm)
Flowers: Single flower growing from each branch on the stem
Habitat: Grassland, meadows, grassy roadsides
Fruits or seeds: Group of small, dry seeds, each with a hooked tip
Flowering time: Spring/summer

Rosebay willowherb

Height: Up to 47 in (120 cm)
Size of flower: 1 in (3 cm)
Flowers: Many flowers growing in a cone shape at the top of the stem
Habitat: Bare or waste ground
Fruits or seeds: White, fluffy seeds
Flowering time: Summer/early fall

Composite flowers

Is my flower head small with white petals? Is the center of my flower head yellow?

Some kinds of flower, such as daisies, are actually made up of hundreds of small flowers. They are called composite flowers. The small flowers form a flower head that looks like a single flower. Only the outer flowers have a single large petal.

White petal

Yellow center

Spotting composite plants

🌼 Some flowers, such as daisies, can open and close their flowers. As the sun sets, the flowers close up tightly. When the sun rises the next morning, the flowers slowly open again.

🌼 A dandelion flower head contains up to 200 tiny flowers. These close up at night or in bad weather.

🌼 The spear thistle is one of the best-protected plants. Each leaf ends in a spine.

Common daisy

Height: 3–6 in (7–15 cm)
Size of flower: 1 in (3 cm)
Flowers: One flower head on each stem
Habitat: Lawns, playing fields, meadows, and roadsides
Fruits or seeds: Small, oval seeds with flat ends, covered in hair
Flowering time: Summer

Purple flower head

Is my flower head yellow? Do all of my tiny flowers have a petal?

Is my flower head purple? Am I tall? Are all my parts spiny?

Hairy seeds

Yellow flower head

Watch it!

Collect some seed heads of dandelion plants—they are called dandelion clocks. Blow on the clock. See how far the seeds travel on their parachutes.

Spiny parts

Dandelion

Height: 2–12 in (5–30 cm)
Size of flower: 3 in (7.5 cm)
Flowers: One flower head on each stem
Habitat: Lawns, grassland, waste ground, and roadsides
Fruits or seeds: Each little seed has a "parachute" of silky hairs, which helps the wind to carry it
Flowering time: Spring/fall

Spear thistle

Height: 12–60 in (30–150 cm)
Size of flower: 2 in (5 cm)
Flowers: One, or a group of two or three flower heads, on a stem
Habitat: Fields, roadsides, waste ground
Fruits or seeds: Yellow seeds with black streaks, topped by a "parachute" of white hairs
Flowering time: Late summer/early fall

Storing food

Some plants have special leaves or stems that are used to store food for winter. Then they will have plenty of food for when they start to grow again in spring. Some of these plants can make new copies of themselves without producing seeds.

Yellow trumpet shape

Does my flower have a yellow trumpet? Does it have quite a few petals and sepals?

Spotting food-storing plants

- A daffodil flower grows from a **bulb**. This is made up of fleshy leaves that are full of food, which is used by the growing shoot.

- A crocus grows from a **corm**. This is a round stem full of stored food.

- A potato is a swollen part of an underground stem, which will grow into a new plant if it is planted.

Daffodil

Height: 8–15 in (20–40 cm)
Size of flower: 1–4 in (3–10 cm)
Flowers: One flower on each flat stem
Habitat: Parks and backyards. Also grows wild in some woods and grassland areas
Fruits or seeds: Fruit splits into three parts when it is ripe, releasing small, brown seeds
Flowering time: Late spring

Drooping
outer petals

Am I small with
funnel-shaped
flowers? Are my
flowers white,
purple, cream,
or yellow?

Flat
stem

Are my
flowers blue
or yellow? Do
I have three
drooping outer
petals? Do
I have a
flat stem?

Funnel-shaped
flower

Flag iris
Height: 15–60 in (40–150 cm)
Size of flower: 3–5 in (8–12 cm)
Flowers: 2–3 flowers on a stem
Habitat: Backyards and parks.
Also grows wild in ditches,
ponds, marshes, and near rivers
Fruits or seeds: Brown seeds
in a pod that splits open
into three parts
Flowering time: Late spring/summer

Crocus
Height: Less than 4 in (10 cm)
Size of flower: 1.5 in (4 cm)
Flowers: One on each stem
Habitat: Parks and backyards.
It grows wild in some areas
Fruits or seeds: Small seeds
inside a three-sided fruit
Flowering time: Late winter/
early spring

Watch it!

Every potato has several
eyes, or buds, from which a
new shoot will grow. Stand a
potato on a sunny windowsill.
Watch what happens to the
"eyes" over a few days.

Climbing plants

Plants need sunlight to make their food. Most plants grow upward to get as much sunlight as possible. Climbing plants with weak stems cannot grow upward on their own. They use other plants for support.

Am I woody with green leaves? Are my leaves heart shaped?

Heart-shaped leaves

Spotting climbing plants

❀ Ivy has tiny roots growing from its stems. These help it to scramble up a tree, fence, or wall.

❀ Honeysuckle climbs by winding itself around young trees. Sometimes it squashes the trunk of the tree and makes it look like a corkscrew.

❀ The long, tough stems of brambles are armed with hooked prickles.

Ivy

Height: Up to 100 ft (30 m) on trees
Size of flower: 0.6 in (4 mm)
Flowers: In groups
Habitat: On trees, cliffs, buildings, walls, and fences
Fruits or seeds: Black fruit
Flowering time: Late fall/early winter

Woody stem

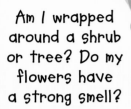

Am I wrapped around a shrub or tree? Do my flowers have a strong smell?

Are my flowers white or pink and do I have blackberries? Am I using sharp, hooked prickles to climb over other plants?

Blackberry fruit

Strong–smelling flower

Blackberry or bramble

Height: Up to 10 ft (3 m)
Size of flower: 1 in (3 cm)
Flowers: Single or in groups
Habitat: Hedgerows, meadows, and woodland
Fruits or seeds: Blackberry fruits
Flowering time: Fall

Honeysuckle

Height: Up to 20 ft (6 m)
Size of flower: 2 in (5 cm)
Flowers: In clusters, or groups, all pointing outward
Habitat: Woodland, hedgerows, and planted in backyards
Fruits or seeds: Groups of red berries
Flowering time: Late summer/early fall

Did you know?

The strangler fig is a climbing plant. It wraps itself around a tree and steals its water and food. Its leaves block the tree's sunlight, causing it to die.

Sharp, hooked prickle

Water plants

All plants need water so they can feed and grow. Water plants grow in places such as ponds, lakes, ditches, and swamps. Some plants live in or under water, while others float on the water's surface.

Do I have large floating leaves? Are my flowers large and white, with 20–25 pointed petals?

Large petal

Spotting water plants

* Plants such as flag irises grow in the shallow water at the edges of ponds, rivers, and streams. They have long, strong roots to fix them firmly in the mud.

* Plants such as water lilies and water crowfoot grow partly covered by water. These plants often have thin and bendy stems so that they can move with the water.

* The stems of some water plants have spaces for air in them. These help to hold the plants up in the water.

White water lily

Height: Grows in water to a depth of about 10 in (3 m)

Size of flower: 4–8 in (10–20 cm)

Flowers: Single flower on a long stem rising from the roots

Habitat: Still or slow–flowing water

Fruits or seeds: Ball-shaped fruits that float away

Flowering time: Summer/ early fall

Yellow center

Am I mostly underwater? Do I have small, white flowers with a yellow center?

Small, white petal

Yellow flower

Water crowfoot

Height: Grows in water to a depth of 1–50 in (2.5–120 cm)
Size of flower: 0.5 in (13 mm)
Flowers: Single or in groups
Habitat: Ponds, streams, rivers, and ditches
Fruits or seeds: Small, dry seeds
Flowering time: Summer

Am I growing in water, but my roots are not in the soil? Are my yellow flowers above the surface of the water?

Bladderwort

Height: Grows in water to a depth of 6–17 in (15–45 cm)
Size of flower: 0.7 in (18 mm)
Flowers: 2–10 flowers on a long stem above the water
Habitat: Deep lakes and ponds
Fruits or seeds: Small, round fruits
Flowering time: Summer

Vital grasses

Grasses are probably the most important plants in the world. They provide food for animals and many of the foods we eat come from grass, too.

Do my flowers look flattened? Do they form a zig–zag pattern up my smooth stem?

Flattened flowers

Zig–zag pattern

Spotting grasses

🌼 Although they are usually dull and green, grasses do have flowers. Grass flowers do not have petals or bright colors because they are pollinated by the wind.

🌼 Grass species include wheat, oats, barley, rice, and maize, which are made into foods such as breakfast cereals and bread.

🌼 Grasses are food for many wild animals. In some places, such as the U.K., straw or reeds are used to make the roofs of houses.

Perennial rye grass

Height: 4–35 in (10–90 cm)
Size of flower: 0.2 in (5 mm)
Flowers: 4–14 flowers in a zig–zag pattern up the stem
Habitat: Grassland, farms, waste ground
Fruits or seeds: Small, dry seeds
Flowering time: Late spring/ early summer

Watch it!

Fill a clean, empty yoghurt cup with cotton balls and pour water on it. Sprinkle grass seeds on the top of the cotton balls in the cup. Water it every day and your seeds will start to sprout.

Am I growing near water? Is my flower head soft and brown in color?

Brown flower

Groups of flowers

Am I growing in a clump with other grass plants? Does my flower head have groups of many flowers?

Oat grass

Height: 20–60 in (50–150 cm)
Size of flower: 0.2 in (6 mm)
Flowers: In loose bunches
Habitat: Rough grassland, meadows, roadsides, hedgerows, and as a weed in corn crops
Fruits or seeds: Small, dry seeds
Flowering time: Summer

Reed grass

Height: 10 ft (3 m)
Size of flower: 0.2 in (6 mm)
Flowers: In large groups
Habitat: Grows in thick clumps on the edges of ponds, lakes, rivers, and marshes
Fruits or seeds: Small, dry seeds
Flowering time: Summer/fall

Trees

A tree is a large, woody plant. Trees grow tall and the branches grow long. At the same time, the roots grow deeper. The tree trunk gets fatter each year as a new layer of wood grows just beneath the bark.

Oak

Height: Up to 115 ft (35 m)
Types of flower: Separate male and female flowers that are green-yellow in color. Male flowers are loose bunches of catkins
Habitat: Parks, large backyards, woodland, and hedgerows
Fruits or seeds: Fruits called acorns grow inside cups
Flowering time: Spring

Acorn

Spotting trees

* Many trees shed their leaves each fall—they are called **deciduous** trees. Not all trees shed their leaves at once—they are called **evergreens**.

* There are about 100,000 different species of tree in the world.

* Trees, such as plum and apple trees, have bright flowers that are pollinated by insects. However, most trees, such as oak, ash, and maple, have flowers that are dull and green and are pollinated by the wind.

Am I large? Does my bark have cracks in it? Are my leaves rounded and do I have acorns?

Common beech

Height: Up to 118 ft (36 m)
Types of flower: Separate male and female flowers that are green-white in color. Single female flowers, and small clusters of male flowers
Habitat: Parks, large backyards, woodland, and hedgerows
Fruits or seeds: Pairs of small, brown nuts in husks
Flowering time: Spring

Pine

Height: Up to 118 ft (36 m)
Types of flower: Separate male and female cones
Habitat: Parks, woodland, large backyards, and forest, mainly in mountain areas
Fruits or seeds: Seeds in cones, which are scattered by the wind
Flowering time: Spring

Nut husk

Ripening cone

Male flower

Is my bark smooth and brown or gray? Are my broad leaves shiny green and do I have nut husks?

Am I evergreen with long needle-shaped leaves? Is my bark red-brown in color?

Strange habits

A few plants have strange feeding habits. Some trap and eat small animals, while some steal food from other plants. There are even plants with flowers that are disguised as something else.

White berry

Am I growing on one of the branches of a deciduous tree? Do I have green leaves and white, sticky berries?

Mistletoe

Height: Up to 35 in (90 cm)
Size of flower: 0.2 in (4 mm)
Flowers: In groups of 3–5
Habitat: Grows on the branches of deciduous trees
Fruits or seeds: Small sticky, white fruit
Flowering time: Fall/winter

Spotting strange habits

❀ Some plants need more than sunlight, water, and soil. They have to eat meat as well. The Venus flytrap has deadly leaves, which help to trap insects.

❀ Some orchids pretend to be flies, bees, or wasps to attract insects to pollinate them.

❀ Mistletoe sinks its special roots into the branches of a tree to get some of its food.

❀ You may not find many strange plants growing in the wild, but they can often be found at garden centers.

Did you know?

The largest meat-eating plant in the world is a kind of pitcher plant. Its flowers can be up to three feet (one meter) deep. It can catch and eat frogs.

"Bumble bee" flower

Green leaf

Am I small and upright? Does each of my flowers look as if it has a bumble bee resting on it?

Bee orchid

Height: 6–24 in (15–60 cm)
Size of flower: Up to 0.7 in (2 cm)
Flowers: Arranged up the stem, with the largest flowers near the bottom
Habitat: On waste ground, grassland, and sand dunes
Fruits or seeds: Tiny black or brown seeds
Flowering time: Mid-summer

Spiky edge

Do I have leaves that form a trap with hairy, spiky edges?

Upright stem

Venus flytrap

Height: Up to 6 in (15 cm), flower stems up to 12 in (32 cm)
Size of flower: 0.7 in (18 mm)
Flowers: Clusters of 3–4 white flowers
Habitat: Boggy areas of Carolina
Fruits or seeds: Small, shiny, black seeds
Flowering time: Late spring

Plants fight back

The leaves, flowers, fruits, and seeds of plants are often eaten by animals. Some plants have special ways of protecting themselves.

Do I have dark-green leaves with spines? Do I have small, white flowers and red berries?

White flower

Red berry

Dark-green leaf

Spotting plant defenders

❀ A large number of plants, including cacti, teasel, thistles, holly, and brambles, use spines or thorns to protect themselves.

❀ A stinging nettle's stems and leaves are covered in tiny needle-like hairs. Below each hair is a tiny bag of poison. If you brush against the nettle plant, the poison is squeezed into your skin, causing a sting.

❀ Some plants, such as foxglove and ragwort, are poisonous to grazing animals. If an animal eats part of the plant, it will be sick or even die.

Holly

Height: Up to 66 ft (20 m)
Size of flower: About 0.2 in (5 mm)
Flowers: In clusters
Habitat: Backyards, hedgerows, and woodland
Fruits or seeds: Red berries
Flowering time: Spring

Do I have leaves that are spoon shaped with rough edges? Am I covered in stinging hairs?

Do I grow tall and straight, with no branches? Are my flowers bell shaped?

WARNING!

Do not touch any of these plants or their berries in case they are poisonous.

Male flower

Bell-shaped flower

Spoon-shaped leaf

Stinging nettle

Height: 12–60 in (30–150 cm)
Size of flower: About 0.1 in (2 mm)
Flowers: Separate male and female plants
Habitat: Hedgerows, waste ground, gardens, woodland, and forests
Fruits or seeds: Tiny, dry seeds
Flowering time: Summer/fall

Foxglove

Height: 25–65 in (60–160 cm)
Size of flower: 2 in (5 cm) long
Flowers: Long spike with 20–80 flowers on a single stem
Habitat: Backyards and parks, hedgerows, woodland, and forests
Fruits or seeds: Seeds in a pod
Flowering time: Summer

Plants in danger

Although plants seem to be almost everywhere, many kinds are in danger of dying out altogether. This is called **extinction**. Plants face extinction because of things that human beings do.

Habitat loss

Every kind of plant lives in particular surroundings. This is its **habitat**. All over the world, habitats are being destroyed. Soil is being covered over with concrete, tarmac, and buildings. When their habitats are destroyed, the plants will have nowhere to grow.

⬆ This land is being cleared to make way for a new factory. Unless the plants that grow here have scattered their seeds to other areas, they will disappear from this area.

Collecting wild plants

In some parts of the world, many beautiful wild plants have been dug up and sold to gardeners. Often the plants can only grow in their original habitats.

⬅ People dug up so many wild orchids to plant in their backyards, the plant is now very rare in the wild.

Pollution

Many plants have been killed by chemicals used on farms and backyards to get rid of pests and kill weeds. Often this type of **pollution** kills not only the weeds, but also harmless wild plants growing nearby. If the chemicals do not kill the wild plants, they may kill the bees and other insects that pollinate them.

↑ The chemical being sprayed on this field may kill trees, flowers, and plants in a nearby hedge or wood.

Did you know?

Some species of orchid can have as many as 20,000 seeds in each capsule. The seeds are so tiny that three million of them only weigh one gram.

Watch it!

Everyone can do their bit to help wild plants by making the areas around homes and schools safe for plants to live. Even without a backyard, we can plant pots, tubs, or window boxes with the flowers that bees, butterflies, and other insects like to visit. It is also important to take care of the soil by not putting anything on it that might damage plants.

Notes for parents and teachers

❀ The children should be encouraged to treat animals with care and respect. Any animals caught for study should be set free in the area they were collected when a project is finished.

❀ When you help a child to identify birds, bugs, and small mammals, bear in mind that only a tiny proportion of the total number of species can be shown in this book. A reference book for the birds, bugs, and small mammals of your local area, illustrated by clear pictures, may be helpful.

❀ Remember when you help a child to identify flowering plants, that only a tiny proportion of the total number of species can be shown in a book of this size. In the world as a whole, there are more than 350,000 species of wild plants, and many thousands more plant species and varieties have been developed to grow in yards.

❀ The children should be encouraged to understand that it is against the law to dig up wild plants without the permission of the owner of the land. In addition, many rarer wildflowers are protected by law.

❀ Before you start wildlife watching, check that the children aren't allergic to any plants or animals.

❀ A visit to a zoo, wildlife park, natural history museum, or butterfly farm will help to show children the great diversity of wildlife in the world today.

- Children should always be accompanied by a responsible adult when wildlife watching.

- Children should not handle living or dead wild birds, as they often are host to disease organisms or parasites. Children should always wash their hands thoroughly after handling food remains, bird feeders, bird baths, or any other items or materials that wild birds have come into contact with.

- If the children collect soil in which to grow seeds or plants, ensure that the soil comes from a part of the yard that has not been contaminated by dog or cat feces and does not contain broken glass, nails, or other sharp objects.

- Remember that some children are allergic to the juices of certain plants. Some children are also allergic to the pollen from flowers.

- Always use plastic jars and other containers in preference to glass ones when collecting plants and bugs.

- A number of safety precautions are necessary when children study invertebrate animals. They should always wash their hands thoroughly after handling small animals, plants, and soil, and particularly before touching food. Similar attention to hygiene is also necessary when cleaning out the boxes in which bugs have been kept.

- Under no circumstances should children handle living or dead wild mammals, since they often are host to disease organisms or parasites. They should always wash their hands thoroughly after handling food remains, or any other materials that wild mammals have come into contact with.

- Bees, wasps, and ants can give painful stings or bites, so do not go near their nests or hives.

- Buy a bug box and put it in your yard or playground. It will give shelter to insects, such as ladybugs, in winter.

Even simple, inexpensive binoculars will help to make birds appear nearer. Children will need help at first in focusing the binoculars and in learning to look through them.

After plaster of Paris casts of footprints have been made and dried (page 73), they can be cleaned with a small soft brush and then painted, using one color for the actual print and another for the background.

Look for tracks and traces of bugs around your area, such as leaves that have been chewed by butterfly larvae (caterpillars). In damp weather, children might be able to see slug trails on footpaths.

Visit a wooded area during late summer or early fall. Bugs are most active at this time of the year.

A simple bird table or bird feeder is quite easy for a child to make, with adult help, or relatively inexpensive to buy. Such bird tables and bird feeders provide an excellent way for children to study common birds closely.

Many mammals are active only at night. It is possible to watch such nocturnal animals with the help of a flashlight fitted with a red filter made of transparent red plastic or cellophane, or by coating the bulb of the flashlight with red ink or layers of the dye from a red pen. Humans can see rather well in red light but nocturnal animals cannot, and are not aware that they are being illuminated.

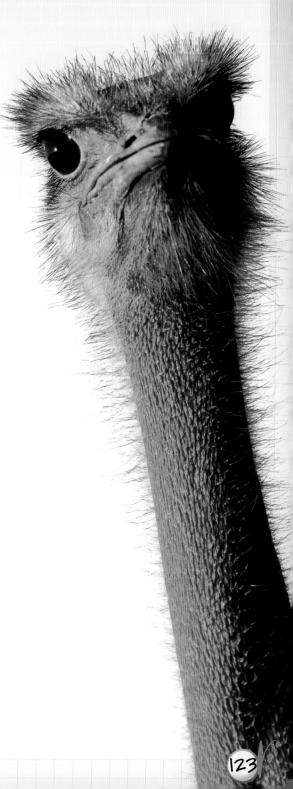

❀ Some useful websites for more information:
www.kidsplanet.org
www.sciencespot.net
www.butterflywebsite.com
www.buglife.org.uk/discoverbugs
www.butterflyconservation.org/text/8/learn.html
www.bbc.co.uk/nature
www.enchantedlearning.com/subjects/birds/
www.kidwings.com/index.htm
www.rspb.org.uk
www.birdwatchin.com/birding_for_kids
http://kids.yahoo.com/animals
www.nwf.org/wildlife
www.sandiegozoo.org
http://www.zsl.org/education/
www.urbanext.uiuc.edu/gpe/
www.picadome.fcps.net/lab/currl/plants/default.htm
http://library.thinkquest.org/3715/
www.inhs.uiuc.edu/resources/tree_kit/student/index.html
www.sciencespot.net
www.kidzone.ws

Glossary

Antenna Feeler on an insect's head used for touching and smelling.

Bulb The underground stem that contains stored food.

Burrow An underground shelter dug by an animal.

Camouflage A way of hiding in which the animal looks like its surroundings.

Carpel The female parts of a flower.

Carrion The flesh of dead animals.

Colony A group of animals of the same species living together.

Corm The swollen part of a stem that grows underground.

Deciduous Trees and bushes that lose their leaves in a certain season.

Den The home of a wild animal.

Eaves The space between the walls and the roof of a building.

Evergreen Trees that do not lose their leaves in a certain season.

Extinction Not in existence any more. A species is extinct when no members of it are left alive.

Feral A pet or farm animal that now lives in the wild.

Fertile In a good condition, or full of nutrients, for plants or animals to grow.

Fertilization When a pollen grain reaches and joins with an egg-cell in a plant. Only a fertilized egg-cell can grow into a seed.

Flock A group of birds.

Forewing The front wing in a pair, or set, of wings.

Habitat Where a plant or animal lives.

Hibernate To spend winter in a sleepy state.

Honeydew A sweet liquid produced by some insects.

Invertebrate An animal without a backbone.

Litter A group of mammal babies born at the same time.

Migration The long journey animals make, at certain times, in search of food, a warmer climate, or somewhere to breed.

Molehill A heap of soil produced from time to time, as a mole digs its tunnel under the ground.

Nectar A sweet-tasting liquid produced by flowers.

Nest The place where a bird lays its eggs.

Nocturnal An animal that is mainly active at night.

Ovary The female part of a flower where the egg-cells and seeds are produced.

Petal One of the brightly colored parts of a flower.

Pollen A yellow dust produced by flowers.

Pollinate To carry pollen from one flower to another.

Pollination The carrying of pollen from one flower to another. This is usually done by insects or the wind.

Pollution Harmful substances that damage the environment.

Predator An animal that lives by hunting other animals.

Prey An animal hunted and eaten by another animal.

Pupa The stage after the grub stage, during which an adult insect develops.

Queen A female ant, bee, or wasp that lays eggs.

Rodent A small animal that has a pair of incisor teeth on both the upper and lower jaw.

Scales Small, flat pieces of skin that overlap each other.

Sepal The special leaf-like part of a flower that covers and protects the bud.

Skeleton The framework of bones inside an animal's body.

Species Any one kind of animal or plant.

Stamen One of the male parts of a flower. A stamen produces pollen.

Stigma The top of the female part of a flower, to which pollen grains stick.

Streamlined Shaped to move smoothly and quickly through air or water.

Style The narrow part of a flower's carpel, which is underneath the stigma.

Talon The claw of a bird of prey.

Wing cases The hard front wings of beetles.

Worker One of the female ants, bees, wasps, or termites that do the work of the colony.

Index